Promoting European dimensions in lifelong learning

Edited by John Field

NIACE

THE NATIONAL ORGANISATION
FOR ADULT LEARNING

Published by the National Institute of Adult Continuing Education
(England and Wales)
21 De Montfort Street, Leicester, LE1 7GE
Company registration no. 2603322
Charity registration no. 1002775
Find the NIACE website at www.niace.org.uk

First published 2002
© NIACE 2002

CATALOGUING IN PUBLICATION DATA
A CIP record for this title is available from the British Library
ISBN 1 86201 048 X

Typeset by Q3 Bookwork, Loughborough
Cover design by Brooke Calverley
Printed in Great Britain by Antony Rowe

Contents

Section III: Involving new learners

Section IV: Changing policies and institutions

Section V: Where to find out more

List of contributors

•

LORE ARTHUR is a lecturer with the Open University in the Faculty of Education and Language Studies where she is involved in the continuing professional development of lecturers in higher education and in the training of foreign language tutors. Her research areas include intercultural communication and comparative adult education, with particular reference to Germany and the UK.

CAROL BLACKMAN is Director of External Relations for the Business School at the University of Westminster. Since the early 1990s she has designed and developed programmes for women returners, especially for highly-qualified women. She teaches marketing strategy on MBA and Postgraduate programmes, and for the School's programmes designed to help women return to work.

JEFF BRIDGFORD is Director of the European Trade Union College. Previously he worked at Heriot-Watt University, Edinburgh (1987–1990) and Newcastle Polytechnic (1979–1987). His books include *The politics of French trade unionism*, Leicester University Press/Pinter, 1991; *Employee relations in Europe* (with John Stirling), Basil Blackwell, 1994; *Biographical dictionary of European labor leaders* (co-editor), Greenwood Press, 1995; and *Trade union education in Europe* (co-editor with John Stirling), ETUCO, 2000.

PAMELA CLAYTON works in the Department of Adult and Continuing Education, University of Glasgow, where she is Research Fellow in adult education and works principally on projects part-funded by the European Commission. She takes an particular interest in groups at risk of social exclusion, particularly ethnic minorities and women.

MARTIN CLOONAN is a lecturer in the Department of Adult and Continuing Education at the University of Glasgow. His main research interests lie in the areas of lifelong learning and popular music.

JANE FIELD established her own consultancy business, Education and Development, in 1994, specialising in education, training and development; project management and evaluation; and community development and capacity building. She has been the Project Manager of four European Union (EU) LEONARDO-funded projects and evaluated many projects funded under EU programmes.

JOHN FIELD has worked in adult education since 1978 and is now Professor of Lifelong Learning at the University of Warwick. Recent books include *European dimensions: Education and training policy and the European Union* (1998) and *Lifelong learning and the new educational order* (2000).

KEITH FORRESTER is a Senior Lecturer in the School of Continuing Education at the University of Leeds. He was the Co-ordinator of recent SOCRATES and a LEONARDO projects.

DAVID FRENCH works in the Centre for Research and Policy in Disability at Coventry University, where he is involved in both research and curriculum activities to improve the knowledge base for disability policy in the higher education sector. His research interests include media policy, in particular, the liberalisation of global trade in cultural production and the relationship between representations of disability and disability policy in the UK and elsewhere in Europe. He is currently working on aspects of sport and disability.

KENNETH GIBSON is an Honorary Fellow in the History Section at Nottingham Trent University. He also teaches history, study skills and personal development at the Centre for Access and Lifelong Learning at the University of Derby.

JENNY HEADLAM-WELLS is European Professional Programmes Manager at the University of Lincolnshire and Humberside. Over the past 10 years she has designed and directed management courses for women graduates returning to their careers. She has also led research projects and published on professional women's career breaks and their return to the labour market. She is a Founder Editor of *The Journal of Gender Studies*.

FRANCES HOMEWOOD has spent 20 years in research and project development, including 5 years as research assistant to David Blunkett, then Leader of Sheffield City Council. Her work has included developing an innovative Paid Educational Leave scheme for low paid Council employees, co-ordinating local authorities in setting up the Local Government Information Unit and establishing a thriving Adult Learners' Week network for Yorkshire television region.

NIGEL LLOYD is a Chartered Civil Engineer and Principal of Cambridge Professional Development, a consultancy organisation involved in many European projects.

SHREE MANDKE works for Cambridge Professional Development, having trained as an Economist at the University of Mumbai and University of Cambridge. Her particular areas of expertise are the development needs of older workers, ethnic aspects of ageing and European funding sources.

LISA MORRIS is Director of International Office at Park Lane College, Leeds. Park Lane College has worked transnationally since 1989 and now works with over 40 partners across 15 European countries. Before joining the College, Lisa worked for a number of years in local government.

IDDO OBERSKI is Lecturer in educational research methods at the University of Glasgow. He has worked in a range of CPD areas in the field of ITE, nursing and management. His current research interest is in thinking skills.

MIKE OSBORNE is Professor of Lifelong Education at the University of Stirling. He is Co-director of the Centre for Research in Lifelong Learning, funded by the Scottish Higher Education Funding Council. He is presently working on a range of research projects on mature student participation for the Department for Education and Skills (DfES) and the Scottish Executive including a comparative study of widening access involving partners in France, Finland, Canada and Australia. He has been active in EUCEN since its foundation.

JOHN PAYNE was Secretary of the International League for Social Commitment in Adult Education from 1989–94. He worked for the Inner London Education Authority from 1983–90. He is currently a Senior Research Fellow in the School of Continuing Education, University of Leeds. As a researcher and writer his main interests are workplace learning and rural adult education, and he also writes on social and political issues. His most recent book is *Journey up the Thames: William Morris and modern England* (2000).

VIDA MOHORČIČ ŠPOLAR is the Director of the Slovenian Institute for Adult Education and became Secretary of the International League for Social Commitment in Adult Education in 1994. Her doctoral thesis at the University of Ljubljana was on Human Resource Development. She is a member of the Steering Committee of the European Society for the Research in the Education of Adults and of the Executive Board of the European Association of Adult Educators. She is also a member of the Governing Board of the UNESCO Institute for Education.

JOHN ROTHERHAM moved to Bristol in 1990 to join Home Farm Trust (HFT) as Personnel Officer. Since 1998 he has been HFT's Head of Personnel and Training for the organisation. His current concerns include employment law, employee participation, change management and, of course, lifelong learning.

JULIE SHAW is the Co-ordinator of the Socrates ALERT project for the Adult and Community Education Service in Bath and North East Somerset Council, which she joined in 1995. She previously co-ordinated a women's education programme and has worked for both Bristol Community Education and Bath Environment Centre. She is helping develop materials and multimedia for teaching and learning for BBC Education Resources and the TUC Learning Services, and is involved in piloting development education with adult learners for the Workers' Education Association (WEA). In 2001 she was awarded a *Winston Churchill Millennium Fellowship* to study the involvement of women in public life at the Woodhull Institute in New York State.

PHILIP TAYLOR is Research Fellow and Director of the Management of Knowledge and Innovation Research Unit in the Open University Business School. He has a research interest in employers' practices and policies respecting older workers.

CHRISTINE TILLSLEY is a Research Consultant working with the Open University Business School. Her previous experience is in the government and voluntary sectors.

PAUL TWYNAM has a background in training for the construction industry and is a Fellow of the CIPD. Paul entered the training profession in 1976, after 17 years in construction he spent 5 years as a freelance trainer working for both commercial and not-for-profit clients. In 1997 he joined the Home Farm Trust as its Management Development Trainer.

SUE WADDINGTON was until 1998 Member of the European Parliament for the East Midlands and chaired the Committee for Education and Culture. She now works for the National Institute of Adult Continuing Education.

1   Building a European dimension: a realistic response to globalisation?

John Field

In recent years, and especially since the mid-1990s, the European Union (EU) has developed an intriguing role in respect of education and training. By the turn of the century, its leaders saw the EU as standing at the leading edge of European policy debates over lifelong learning. It has openly criticised the member states for failing to turn their general lifelong learning policies into practical measures, and launched a far-reaching consultation on the best ways for the EU and its member states to make lifelong learning 'a reality' (CEC 2000).

Nor is its contribution limited to ideas. Through its Structural Funds, the European Commission channels considerable public funding into vocational training programmes in the member states, including significant subsidies to government training for special groups, such as the unemployed. It has developed its own transnational action programmes in both education and training, and it funds transnational research into education and training. Since the mid-90s the Commission has made adult learning a priority in each of these areas. Furthermore, although the member states retain most law-making powers, much European legislation has an indirect impact on adult learning (equal opportunity requirements, and health and safety regulations are good examples). The European Parliament has enthusiastically pushed for co-operation and innovation on adult learning policy. In turn, a growing number of national and cross-European professional interest groups are lobbying the EU's policy bodies on matters related to adult learning. So, as well as our general duty to enlighten and inform, we all have a vested interest in knowing more about the EU.

This book is intended as a resource for professionals in adult learning who want to increase their knowledge of the EU's role in their area, and develop their capacity for benefiting from European programmes. It draws on the rich body of experience that now exists in the UK and elsewhere of working on a cross-European basis. The various chapters describe a range of activities with different types of adult learner, most funded by the EU, and all of them involving a transnational dimension. As well as reflections on experience, the book also brings together lessons that the contributors – all professionals involved in supporting adult learners – have learned from their experiences. It does not cover locally or nationally provided training that is funded from Europe, such as the New Deal or other programmes supported by the European Social Fund (ESF). Although these are certainly important, they do not routinely involve the often dramatic challenges of working on a cross-border basis with colleagues from other European countries. And this is the central focus of the chapters that follow.

The development of EU policies and programmes

We are living in a global village. So we often hear, at any rate. In western Europe, the growing role of the EU has become a key part of the globalisation story. Particularly since the achievement of the Single European Market in 1992, the EU has become a truly significant actor on the world stage. It represents both a response by its members to the pressures of globalisation and is, at the same time, a formidable force for globalisation. Its powers are substantial, encompassing huge areas of economic and social policy, as well as more limited domains in areas such as foreign relations, and its membership is still growing. The EU is still a relatively new and untested force and, as such, it should properly command the attention of professionals concerned with enabling adults to learn how to negotiate their lives in the global village. But there are also more focussed, even sectional, reasons for the EU to command our attention.

In 2001, governments and providers across Europe were invited to respond to a European Commission memorandum on lifelong learning. Not pulling its punches, the memorandum criticised member states for their failure to translate aspirations into concrete measures, concluding that lifelong learning should form the cornerstone for all future education and training policy. The Commission's logic followed a familiar pattern (globalisation, social exclusion, technological change and an ageing population all played their usual part). But to British ears at least, what was striking was not simply the central place that the Commission gave to lifelong learning, and to adult learning in particular. Even more remarkable was the fact that the Commission was not concerned solely with training for competitiveness, but that it placed learning for active citizenship and social inclusion on an equal footing as the goals of a modern Europe.

How did this come about? To some extent, the EU has always had a stake in training and education policy, ever since its foundation in 1957 (Field 1998). However, it was hardly a central area of interest in the early years. For the six countries that created the EU, what mattered was mainly the reduction of barriers to free trade within its borders, together with the protection of European farming from (cheaper) competitors, such as Australia, Canada, the Caribbean and, above all, the USA. Other than the ESF, which acquired its present significant function during the sharp rise in youth unemployment of the 1970s, the EU did relatively little to develop this area of policy until the mid-1980s. This lack of interest only changed when the member states agreed in 1985 to set a clear deadline for the completion of the Single European

Market. This coincided with the appointment of Jacques Delors as a very energetic and visionary President of the European Commission. After 1986, although education and training policy remained subordinate to wider economic concerns, interest in education and training rose steadily to the top of the EU policy agenda.

Initially, the Commission identified education and training largely as an adjunct to economic policy. Its main interest in promoting programmes was in helping to support the mobility of labour, which – along with the mobility of goods, capital, and services – was a keystone of the Single European Market process. In the early stages, the Commission undertook two broad sets of programmes. First, it launched a series of programmes that offered funding incentives to education and training institutions to develop transnational partnerships. Because the Union's role in education was severely limited at that time, its ERASMUS programme – promoting staff and student exchanges in higher education – was, for legal purposes, defined as in the area of vocational training. Only after the Treaty on European Union, which was approved by the member states at Maastricht in 1992, was the EU able to develop policies and programmes for the entire education sector. By 1995, the Commission was able to launch two new comprehensive programmes: LEONARDO, covering transnational projects in vocational training; and SOCRATES, with a similar role in respect of education.

The second area of interest before 1992 was in the mutual recognition of qualifications across Europe. The Commission was able to use its legal powers in vocational training to legislate on the recognition of qualifications, passing two General Directives in the late 1980s that covered degrees and professional qualifications. Member states are required to transpose Commission Directives into national legislation, so that, in these particular cases, qualifications gained in any one member state must be recognised across the EU. In the event, relatively few citizens have made use of this right, which turned out to be of largely symbolic significance.

In addition to these two sets of policy instruments, the EU also pursued its growing interest in education and training by other means. Right across the Commission's policies and programmes for social affairs, employment and research and technology development, there was growing attention to the role of education and training. Particularly important here were the Community Initiatives, a set of employment and social priorities funded through the Structural Funds, which have now been brought together within the EQUAL programme. These included:

- ADAPT – aimed at helping retrain workers at risk from industrial restructuring
- NOW – programmes to widen vocational opportunities for women

- INTEGRA – aimed at those who are otherwise excluded from the labour market
- HORIZON – aimed at people with disabilities.

Increasingly, projects funded under the Community Initiatives have required transnational partnerships. In some respects then, the EQUAL initiative makes similar demands for European collaboration in the better-known education and training programmes, SOCRATES and LEONARDO.

In addition to the early concern with promoting labour mobility, under Delors' leadership the Commission started to turn its attention to the role of education and training in creating a common sense of European identity among the continent's young people. Much of the emphasis on transnational activity came to be justified by reference to its role in promoting a 'citizen's Europe', by allowing teachers, trainers and learners to travel and work with their fellow-Europeans. Citizenship development has been particularly important for adult education projects, many of which have been created by voluntary sector providers. By the mid-1990s, the EU had considerably broadened its stake in education and training, and was starting to show growing interest in promoting lifelong learning.

Lifelong learning at the centre?

In 1994, Jacques Delors presented the Commission with a White Paper on employment policy (CEC 1994). In agreeing to publish the White Paper, the Commission endorsed a proposal for a European Year of Lifelong Learning, which followed in 1996. Subsequently, the Commission also issued a White Paper on education and training, significantly subtitled *Towards the Learning Society* (CEC 1995). These three public steps – two White Papers and a designated Year of Lifelong Learning – marked a substantial shift in thinking within the Commission, which increasingly placed lifelong learning at the centre of its policies and programmes for education and training. This was also reflected by the importance placed on lifelong learning right across the LEONARDO programme for vocational training, and the decision to create an Adult Education Action within the framework of SOCRATES (Nuissl 1999).

The central place of lifelong learning became clear when the Commission published its early proposals for the SOCRATES and LEONARDO programmes for the period 2000–2006. Significantly, the Commission chose the title *Towards a Europe of Knowledge* to sum up its proposals, which it went on to justify as an attempt to 'make a reality of the idea of lifelong learning, which was at the heart of the European Year devoted to this theme' (CEC 1997, 3). It then returned to the topic in 2000, with the publication of a *Memorandum on Lifelong Learning*, which called on member states to debate and respond to what it called 'six basic messages' (CEC 2000, 4), concerning the role in lifelong learning of:

- New basic skills for all, including social competence, enterprise and foreign languages, which the Commission argued to be as necessary today as more conventional basic skills, such as literacy, numeracy and IT competence, were in the past.
- Higher investment levels in human resources.
- Innovation in methods of teaching and learning, including wider application of the new ICT.
- Recognition of learning, including a greater value upon learning from experience and in informal settings.
- Rethinking the role of careers guidance and educational advice, with a focus on locally accessible sources of information.
- Bringing learning and learners closer together, both through ICT applications and the development of local opportunities.

Once again, the Commission spoke of its ambition to make real progress towards lifelong learning, making explicit its judgement that member states had so far made limited concrete progress towards implementation of what was a widely agreed policy objective.

Of course, the Commission might also be found wanting if judged by the same criteria. Its publications on lifelong learning have often been long on rhetoric, but short on specifics. This is particularly so when it comes to the Commission's own programmes. Perhaps this reflects in part two factors that tend to ensure that education and training systems continue to divide along national fault lines. The first is that legal responsibility for education policy, and for much vocational training policy, remains with the member states, so that the EU's influence is often indirect, rather than direct. The second is that, although workers are technically free to roam across the European labour market in search of work, the fact is that, for whatever reason, few do so (and most of those few tend, like the Irish in Britain, to move along well-established pathways).

Moreover, the very nature of the Commission's programmes has tended to limit their impact. Few mobility programmes are accessible to adult students, particularly if they have jobs or caring responsibilities (though, as several chapters here show, a bit of ingenuity can sometimes help adults to abandon their other commitments for a brief period). The principle of matched funding may pose particularly difficult challenges to small firms and voluntary organisations, unless their business is vocational training, in which case the European grant may well represent an additional income stream. The value of activity on a cross-border basis is often hard to demonstrate convincingly. Many of the Commission's pilot projects have been criticised as tantamount to reinventing wheels, then describing the process in badly-worded English. In general, the Commission has often shown itself remarkably unreflective where its own activities are concerned. Evaluation procedures within the Commission are designed solely for organisational accounting, rather than determining the wider impact of its activities, and examining what has been learned. And in some cases, the lessons have been frankly negative. Nevertheless, as the chapters here show, the opportunities are real enough, and the potential benefits are considerable.

So what is to be done?

The relevance of the European dimension for those concerned with adult learning is easy to summarise:

- As the EU has grown in power and influence, so all of Europe's adults require new skills and knowledge to be effective citizens.
- Cross border mobility in Europe requires us to reflect on our values and those of our neighbours.
- Internationalisation of goods and service, particular inside what is now an open European economic area, broadens the basis of vocational training.
- European legislation covers many areas where training is now a regulatory requirement (these include equal opportunities, occupational health and safety, and environmental regulation).
- The EU has both direct and indirect influence on education and training policies.
- The EU controls a small, but still significant, proportion of funding allocated to training and, to a much lesser extent, education.
- European-wide organisations and networks have grown up that represent the interests of those who work with adult learners.

The chapters in this volume seek to show just how this agenda might be taken forward.

The authors come from a range of different organisational backgrounds, and work with an enormous variety of adult learners, but all share in common the fact that they are experienced practitioners. In each case, they have tried to draw wider lessons from their experiences, and formulate them in ways that might help colleagues interested in developing a European dimension in other settings. Many of the lessons have drawn upon failures, as well as successes, and as editor I would particularly like to emphasise the open and honest manner in which the contributors have agreed to share information and ideas that more self-serving individuals might have wished to keep to themselves. The contexts described here vary from very localised activities, to ambitious attempts at creating international networks of like-minded practitioners; from the face-to-face world of supporting and advising learners, to the development of remote systems for supporting learning through the new technologies.

It is certainly easy enough to poke fun at the educational free-riders on the European gravy train. In his column in *The Times Higher Education Supplement*,

Laurie Taylor once imagined a spoof 'European Conference on the Evaluation of European Conferences on European Co-operation in the European Community'. The programme included workshops on 'Completing expenses forms for European conferences: problems and prospects' and 'Staff exchanges between European countries: avoiding Belgium' (Taylor, 1995). All very droll, and clearly there are partnerships and projects that have only won support because of their timing. The Commission's policy – acquired under Delors – of promoting contact between European educators as a policy goal in its own right is not sustainable. If it does not fall victim to the Commission's own attempts at improving its long-term effectiveness, it is unlikely to survive the pressures of the EU's plans for a wider membership. But, as the programmes described here confirm, European partnerships can be a promising way of enriching the curriculum, developing staff, and building an outward-looking organisational strategy. Of course it can be fun, and rewarding, and damned hard work.

If well conceived and carefully managed, the European dimension can bring enormous benefits to all concerned. As the independent evaluators reviewing the early years of the Adult Education Action in SOCRATES concluded, despite some failures, overwhelmingly:

> the projects proved to be a gold mine for innovation and good practice in many respects. Outstanding results have been achieved, especially in the development of new teaching and learning methodologies, in the improvement of European co-operation, networking and mutual exchange of experience and ideas. Considerable contributions have also been made to an increased understanding concerning problems of key significance to our society, such as environmental issues or questions of racism and xenophobia (Nuissl 1999, 13).

At the very least, what is involved is an opportunity for benchmarking against current practice elsewhere (CEC 1999). It is also, as Sue Waddington reminds us in her chapter, a robust basis for engaging with the policy makers at European level (who are not, as she points out, quite as remote as they might sometimes seem). Most ambitiously, the European dimension represents our most practicable hope of building an effective educational and training response to the globalising processes that now affect all areas of social, economic and cultural life.

References

CEC (1994) *Employment, Growth, Competitiveness*, Office for Official Publications, Commission of the European Communities

CEC (1995) *Teaching and Learning: Towards the Learning Society*, Office for Official Publications, Commission of the European Communities

CEC (1997) *Towards a Europe of Knowledge*, Commission of the European Communities

CEC (1999) *Transnationality Works! If you work at it*, Office for Official Publications, Commission of the European Communities

CEC (2000) *Memorandum on Lifelong Learning*, Commission of the European Communities

Field, J. (1998) *European Dimensions: Education, Training and the European Union*, Jessica Kingsley

Nuissl, E. (ed) (1999) *Adult Education and Learning in Europe: Evaluation of the Adult Education Action within the SOCRATES Programme*, Deutsches Institut für Erwachsenenbildung, Frankfurt am Main

Taylor, L. (1995) *The Times Higher Education Supplement*, 5 May 1995

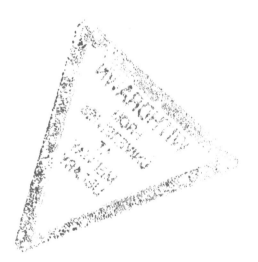

Section I
Learning lessons

2   Developing and writing proposals for European funding

Jane Field

Context – why bother?

Writing a successful bid for funding is an art in itself. Some people seem to get it right every time and others don't. This paper is based on a great deal of experience of writing and reviewing bids for European funding, most of them successful, as well as evaluating a wide range of European-funded activities. What have been the key lessons? Broadly, although there can be no automatic guarantee of success, there are some basic rules and approaches that I find helpful in writing proposals.

The benefits of a European dimension

In 1999, I undertook a survey of current practice on behalf of the Universities Association for Continuing Education's European network. Almost all the higher education institutions (HEIs) reported some transnational continuing education activity. The main reasons given for embarking on this work included:

- Contributing to an international research base and other research opportunities;
- Access to new ideas coming out of Europe;
- Opportunities to exchange and expand knowledge;
- Benefits to students and staff participating in mobility programmes;
- Raising the institutional profile;
- Networking, developing new contacts and partnerships.

For those working with adults, then, the institutional benefits are potentially substantial.

The survey also asked about benefits to individual staff. Many of the responses focused on networking:

- Sharing experiences, good practice and knowledge;
- Working in partnership with people who have similar interests;
- The chance of working together again in the future;
- A greater understanding of education and training systems in other European countries.

The implications from these responses are that individuals working in continuing education gained from participating in transnational partnerships.

Other more general benefits of receiving funding from European Union (EU) programmes included:

- The opportunity to try something new;
- Being able to take some risks and diversify existing activity;
- Looking at things from a slightly different or wider perspective through meeting with transnational partners;
- Recognising that in the partnerships there tend to be those whom you benefit with your experience and others who you learn from;
- A funding source for our ideas.

While not all the feedback was positive, on balance people felt that the gain was worth the trouble. Very often European funding makes it possible to diversify or expand an existing area of development, or activity within the organisation. Having run a related project on a local or regional basis gives a useful insight into the tasks and issues that the transnational project would need to address at the outset. If the programme criteria match something that you are doing, and offer the chance to diversify, innovate, and reach different markets; and if there is real benefit or opportunity to be gained from a European dimension – then submitting a proposal for EU funding is likely to be worth taking further.

Finding basic information and meeting like-minded people

How do you take the first steps to become an active participant in EU programmes? The ideas and checklists offered below are not a guarantee for success; however, they do offer useful 'tips' (all of which have been used in practice) to help with writing the funding proposal.

First, find out more. A lot of information is available on the internet (see the chapter on Resources), including websites for all the main programmes and for the Education and Culture Directorate. European Documentation Centres, European Infopoints and some libraries will have the *Official Journal of the European Communities*, which gives information on Council Decisions and 'Calls for Proposals' for programmes. Such information can be dry, and provides no insights whatever into what it is like to actually participate in an EU project. What it will do is give the official background, eligibility criteria and objectives of the different programmes. There are also a number of commercial organisations who provide updates on new and existing programmes (for a fee), either based on a specific sector (eg HEIs) or a particular activity (eg cultural and arts programmes). Most projects have directories listing previous projects, and some have a newsletter.

Second, get to know some potential partners. There are formal and informal ways of looking for likely partners. Some National Agencies have a good reputation for supporting the partner search activity – for example the Finnish National Agency will send out mailings to those who have registered an interest. There are events, such as exhibitions and conferences, where bulletin boards or National Agency stands allow people seeking partners to post a short message. You can spot those who are old hands at this activity – they will bring a typed description of their areas of interest and identify a time and place to get together. If you are planning to attend one of these events, it helps to do some preparation beforehand. Think about subject areas, elements of curriculum development or target groups with whom you want to work within a European dimension. Always have plenty of business cards available to hand out! Some people prepare a one page summary of their ideas for a project.

Informal networking can be very effective, but some people find it hard to get into what feels like an invisible club. It is usually possible to join a European network of people who share professional interests similar to your own, without necessarily having to participate right away in a project. A wide variety of Europe-wide associations and groupings cover different aspects of adult education, vocational training, and community development (some relevant websites are listed in the Resources chapter). Some are relatively formal, with invited members, while others are more open and inclusive. Participating in a network is a relatively simple way of meeting people who are involved in EU projects. It offers opportunities to find out first-hand what the experience really is like; and many project partnerships involve people who originally met and got to know each others' professional interests through European networks or through attendance at transnational conferences. Such activities imply a need to invest some time in building contacts and knowledge prior to bidding for or receiving funding to support projects. However, some mobility projects (including GRUNTDVIG and other SOCRATES programmes, for example) will fund pre-exploratory visits to meet with potential partners, prior to submitting the full proposal.

Developing a proposal

Having identified a number of potential partners you need to think about further developing the proposal. Many Commission programmes ask interested projects to submit a pre-project proposal. This involves providing an outline of your project and the partners, leaving the full application form until an initial evaluation has been carried out. Before submitting the pre-proposal it is helpful to write a two-page summary; including objectives, deliverables and evidence supporting the need for the project. Many National Agencies are happy to look over and comment on this at the outset; and can indicate if the idea does or does not meet with the ethos behind the programme. This document can also be useful for initially briefing potential partners.

You need to decide which partners are going to take on which roles – and particularly, what responsibilities you will acquire. Above all, as you are thinking about writing a bid, bear in mind the possibility that if you succeed, your organisation may end up as Project Contractor, with you leading the project. As Contractor, the responsibilities for implementing the proposal will lie with you and your organisation. Unless you have the resources and support for this, you may be better off as a partner in someone else's project. Tactically, bear in mind that, within some programmes, there is the possibility that the bid will have a greater chance of success if it is submitted to a National Agency in one of the other partner countries (many programmes are over-subscribed in the UK, or receive a higher number of applications from the UK than other countries).

One lesson from the experience of others is that you need to identify at the outset exactly why you want to get involved in the first place – and why it will appeal to your organisation. No one has got rich from taking part in a European project! EU projects require matched funding, and usually need substantial amounts of time, enthusiasm and other resources. Most people will tell you that they end up putting in more time than they budgeted for, and it is not unusual that they will considerably exceed the original level of matched funding from their organisation.

Finding out more about the programme

Having decided that you are proceeding with a proposal, you need to find out as much as you can about the EU programme. There are a wide variety of resources that can be used to find out information on any given EU-funded programme. If you have a low tolerance for information overload, or cannot stand jargon and technical terminology, this is the time to think about giving up! If you have the stamina to persist, then take the time to look at the most important of the documents available, as this will provide a better overview of the programme and its main aims. It should also give you a picture of what has been funded previously within the programme (or similar programmes, if this one is new).

Early planning, before you even start the task of writing the proposal, should include a review of the following:

- The formal call for proposals, published in the *Official Journal of the European Communities*;
- The programme application pack and the so-called *Vademecum* (basically, a guide to the programme and application procedures);
- A skim through directories of previous projects funded under the programme (if available).

Much of this information is found on the EU's official website, which will also have other material that can be trawled if you want an in-depth knowledge of the background. For example, you may find it useful to look over copies of speeches by Commissioners, or browse through relevant press releases. If you know anyone who has already been involved in the programme, or one of its predecessors, now is a good time to buy them a cup of coffee, and pick their brains.

Having thoroughly reviewed the range of documentation, I usually find it useful to make a list of the key words and note the core programme objectives. The key words will help focus on the central question: is this for me? You can also use them later when you come to write your application. Above all, check the eligibility criteria – make sure that what you want to do fits (eg focus of the funding, number of partners, types of partners). And check the deadline for pre-proposals and proposals. Although it may be a couple of months or more away, there are plenty of time-consuming tasks to be completed. In my experience, two days before the deadline there are always people sitting at their desks, sending email and faxes to potential partners, in an attempt to secure all the information required to send off the proposal in time to meet the deadline.

By now, you should have enough information to decide whether developing a bid is worth your while. It is seldom advisable to submit a proposal for something that is completely new to your organisation. However, if you are already developing an activity that links to the programme criteria, it may well be worth looking at this as a potential funding opportunity that can add value to what you are already achieving – for example, by helping you to expand, diversify, reach new markets, improve quality, consolidate your reputation or open new doors in an area in which you already have an interest. You should by now be in a position to 'determine the justification and scope' (Churchouse and Churchouse 1999) of the project. This includes identifying deliverables and benefits; what the project will encompass (and what it will not), constraints and limitations, and the project stakeholders.

Finding partners

Finding partners is a very imprecise science, it can also be very difficult. There is no magic formula for getting it right and identifying a 'good' partner. Sometimes, with even the best planning, it may be simply down to the group dynamics and personal chemistry as to whether the partnership will work or not. Nevertheless, experience suggests that there are some basic rules of thumb; and that finding partners for transnational projects involves many of the same skills and procedures as does building a locally based partnership.

Nuissl has rightly pointed out that although finding the right partners 'requires a lot of time and effort', working with the partnership will certainly affect the outcomes of the project (Nuissl 1999). Experience shows that ideally the person bringing the partnership together (who, in practice, is usually the person writing the bid, and will end up as the contractor and/or project manager) will have personally met all the partners beforehand. This may be through attending conferences, networks or other events across Europe. Alternatively, someone else in the organisation may have made contact with potential partners, or better still have previously worked with them. A less reliable introduction is through a trusted colleague, who knows of another person/organisation with similar interests. If it is not possible to meet in person, the most risky option is to choose a partner through a paper-search. Such a search may be done, for example, by contacting a National Agency, reading a Year Book, or simply scanning the literature from previous projects and noting where someone has expressed an interest in a similar area to the one you are involved in.

There can also be an element of luck. I have been in the fortunate position of asking a colleague in Ireland to recommend someone with an interest in the project proposal that I was developing, and being given the name of a contact in Dublin who turned out to be a diligent, responsible and generally ideal partner. In contrast, I have evaluated a project where the contractor, who was also responsible for project management, visited all the partners before submitting the application, but ended up with a group that didn't ever gel throughout the 2 year project. Building trust takes time, and can be a complicated process. A survey of adult education projects in the SOCRATES programme found that 'becoming acquainted with the partners took more time than they had foreseen', though it was expected that this process would become smoother as adult educators became accustomed to transnational activities (Nuissl 1999, 45–6).

When planning the partnership it is necessary to take the programme eligibility criteria into account. Above all, check the number of member countries that need to be involved. There are occasions when it is beneficial to identify whether there are any advantages in targeting particular countries (ie countries who are 'flavour of the month'), a current example is to include at least one of the pre-accession countries. Certainly, when developing the partnership, there is value in seeking to get a good balance across the European countries; for example, including partners from northern, southern and central/eastern Europe. It may be worthwhile inviting someone from a new member state to participate (provided of course that they meet the criteria you have in mind for your partners), as they tend to be under-represented in existing projects. The Commission has also negotiated bilaterally with the Association States (that is, those who are to join the EU) and third countries, such as Australia and Japan, so that they can participate in some programmes. But don't go over the top. Think carefully before becoming over-ambitious; it might look good on paper to have partners from ten different countries – but how effective and how manageable will this be in practice?

For many Commission programmes, partnerships need to include a mix of different types of organisation. In these cases, partnerships comprised solely of educational institutions are less likely to succeed, or sometimes are explicitly ruled ineligible. The programme eligibility criteria will identify the partners that the Commission requires, usually a mix of educational, private and public organisations. For some programmes, the Commission will expect to see evidence that the 'social partners' are involved; this refers to trade unions and employer organisations. A good tactic can be to have two different types of partner organisations from four or five different countries.

Foundations for partnership

Churchouse and Churchouse (1999) offer four helpful questions to ask about project stakeholders:

- What do they bring to the project?
- What do they get from the project?
- Are they likely to be supportive, neutral or hostile?
- How will you involve them?

It is worth bearing these questions in mind at each stage of the proposal, but they will be particularly relevant in identifying why you are proposing this particular group of partners, and what you want to say about the partnership in the proposal itself. Most project proposals expect you to provide a brief summary for each of the partner organisations, and this could be a useful framework to use when writing this section.

The checklist below gives a list of more detailed considerations to be taken into account, particularly at the stage of writing the application, whilst firming up the partnership (Field 1997). By the time that they are signed up to the project, partners should have an understanding and demonstrated agreement about a number of general principles:

- An interest in learning new skills and meeting challenges;
- A common philosophy and values;
- An involvement in promoting and encouraging European integration and knowledge of other cultures;
- A belief in partnership as a way of working;
- A compatible range and level of activities, professional knowledge and experience;
- A compatible approach to innovation.

It is worth considering what evidence you have gathered to show whether your potential partners will be able to work together, and will be committed to the project? One basic test is whether partners are replying to your requests for information whilst you are at the proposal development stage.

In deciding to co-operate, the partners need to agree on the following practical matters:

- Written clarification of the purposes of the project;
- Clear understanding of the transnational activities to be undertaken;
- Realistic and innovative attitudes to transnational partnerships and co-operation;
- A common vision of what they can expect from and contribute to possible projects;
- Opportunity and commitment to financially resource projects (including formally agreeing to providing matched funding);
- Common working language(s) at meetings and in project documentation;
- Commitment at senior management level;
- Clearly identified roles and responsibilities for the individuals involved.

If at any stage the partners do not seem to be committed when developing the project, and cannot (or do not) respond to requests for information, this may suggest that they will prove difficult to work with in the future. Each potential partner should be asked to explain why they want to be involved in the project, and what experience and expertise they can bring. At a later stage in the proposal-writing process, partners will need to send a formal 'letter of intent', showing their involvement in the project and the financial breakdown (ie EU funding contribution and the matched funding from their organisation). This letter must be signed by a senior officer in the organisation; this not only meets the programme criteria, but also demonstrates that the organisation (in principle at least) supports involvement in the project.

Finally, you should get to know the track record of all the partner organisations. Most proposals will include a question about partner involvement in previous EU projects, so you will need to have this information anyway. In general, those who have worked on successful projects (both EU and national) in the past are likely to make good partners, while those who have worked on unsuccessful projects may have learned some valuable lessons, but could have a poor reputation with the Commission. Bear in mind that success, in this context, means that the Commission is satisfied with the outcomes, and not whether the outcomes have had the desired impact!

Writing the bid: identifying tasks

Writing a project proposal can be an opportunity to reflect and learn. It can also be frustrating, time-consuming, and exhausting – you won't be the first person to wonder why on earth you are spending your time writing a proposal for a European project. Again, there is no simple recipe for success, but the tips below are based on a great deal of experience, as well as sheer common sense.

First, the project proposal will require clear evidence of need. I usually start by looking for relevant statistics and quotes from policy documents or research findings relevant to the proposal. Evidence of need for the project should not just be taken from the national viewpoint of the UK, but ought to include examples from all partner countries. A second source is evidence that this project is relevant to the EU's own priorities. Publications produced by the European Commission (particularly White Papers, Commission memoranda, research sponsored by the Commission, programme reports and evaluation studies) are often a fruitful source.

The next step is to outline the project itself. Key issues to address at the project planning stage include:

- Clear objectives;
- The proposed time-scale;
- The team of people;
- The nature of innovation (and its extent);
- The creation of change – and its sustainability.

(adapted from Reiss 1992)

When writing the proposal a good starting point is to break the project down into small components. These components should include all specific tasks, and address who will carry them out. The list below shows some of the tasks that you might need to include:

- Project management (more on this below);
- Administration;
- Mailing lists;
- Research (eg surveys, action research, questionnaire analysis, interviews);
- Delivering specific activities;
- Developing learning materials;
- Piloting materials or other products;
- Promotional materials;
- Report writing;
- Financial procedures;
- Hosting partner meetings;
- Translation;
- Dissemination activity (more on this below);
- Evaluation.

Proposals must show that the project is genuinely transnational. This means showing that all the partners from all the countries involved will be actively contributing to and participating in the project. One way of showing roles and tasks for each partner is to produce a matrix, with the partners on one axis and activities on the other. Producing the list of tasks and asking partners how they will contribute is a simple way of producing such a matrix, which can then feature in the project application. The transnational dimension of the partnership must also be reflected in the financial budget for the project, showing how project funding will be distributed among the partners.

The working language for the project needs to be agreed by all partners when the proposal for funding is being written. Many projects use English as the working language for all documents and meetings, even in projects where none of the partners is a native English speaker, as it is the language most common to the partners involved (there is a further discussion of this issue in Lore Arthur's chapter). But even though you have agreed on a working language for the partnership, the activities will need to be delivered in the languages of the partner countries. Lack of funding for translation (for written materials, or spoken translation) within the European programmes is a problem. Professional translation is expensive, and few have found computer translation packages of acceptable quality. Some projects sub-contract translation to non-specialists at a reduced fee. In the case of postgraduate students, for example, translation work is often undertaken, at least partly, in exchange for a public statement of their role in any products, which can be useful for their future career. Don't assume that postgraduates are the best writers in the world; their work should be edited by another native speaker.

Linguistic confusion, although a constant risk, can usually be kept to a minimum. Ensure at the outset that everyone understands what key words mean. This can be revisited at the first partner meeting, but is worth taking into account when writing the proposal. Avoid colloquialisms, and explain all acronyms. Bear in mind that the selection committee judging your proposal may not include any native English speakers.

Project management

In the majority of bids the Project Contractor takes on management responsibilities. While this is not always the case, project management cannot be subcontracted and must be done by one of the partner organisations. Proposals must describe project management, identifying key tasks to be performed by the project management team. Project management roles include:

- Progress chasing;
- Report writing;
- Financial reporting;
- Communication with the Commission;
- Maintaining regular contact with the partners;
- Cheer-leading and motivating;
- General administration (eg booking flights, booking hotels, chasing partners for information, minute taking and circulating);
- Monitoring, evaluation and review.

Planning the partner meetings is also the responsibility of the project management team. To ensure shared ownership, it is best to hold partner meetings in a different partner's country on each occasion; host partners usually help with domestic arrangements in their own countries. This can be included in the matrix of partner roles and responsibilities (mentioned above). Three or four full partner meetings are usually needed over a 2 year project; and these need to be effective, given that during the project's lifetime the partners will probably only meet together for 12–15 days. Each partner meeting will have a different (and clearly identified) focus, and the group dynamics will be at a different stage at each meeting; this needs to be considered during the planning stage.

Communication is an issue for any partnership. It can be difficult enough to communicate effectively within local partnerships, and communication issues are even more crucial where face-to-face meetings are infrequent. The partners need to identify and agree at the first meeting how they would like to communicate – and the methods used should subsequently be reviewed. Some of the options I have found effective are listed in Table One. Keep communication simple and don't place unrealistic burdens on partners.

Finally, in the project management section of the proposal it may be appropriate to identify smaller working groups to take forward specific elements of the project. Using working groups encourages partners to actively communicate and bring their personal skills, resources and expertise to the project. It may also encourage partners to enter into dialogue with other representatives of their own organisation. It can also lead to difficulties, of course, if some partners feel excluded from an activity that interests them, or that their expertise is being ignored. This therefore needs sensitive handling, and any sub-group should understand that it is accountable to the wider partnership. Transnational partners often enjoy working in smaller groups and find that it promotes greater confidence and trust, facilitating greater exchange of ideas and feelings of ownership and involvement.

Dissemination

All programmes require that project lessons are disseminated. The Commission likes to see evidence that dissemination is being taken seriously from the start – which means that all work-stages of the project need to include dissemination as a partner activity, and it should be an agenda item at all partner meetings. Dissemination can be about both the process and the products. Ideally, methods should be affordable, accessible, attractive, and adaptable for translation.

Dissemination may be to a range of different audiences; including immediate stakeholders, European Commission and National Government Agencies,

Table 1: Communications in transnational partnerships

Method of communication	Advantages	Disadvantages
Email	Immediacy Cost-effective Encourages prompt response Useful for monthly update from project manager Everyone has received the same information May be filed and used in audits	Make sure all partners have access (most will) Check acceptable standards for sending/receiving attachments
Telephone	Personal Useful as a second resort when progress-chasing Once the person is contacted there is the chance of getting an immediate reply	Many people find it harder to speak a non-native language on the telephone than face-to-face
Telephone conferencing	Useful when used to discuss a specific issue Effective when well-chaired	Can be intimidating for those who are less confident Language can be more difficult on the telephone Ineffective for general discussion
Video-conferencing	Saves on travel time Partners have a visual image	Can be expensive Can be unreliable Access may not be easily available to all partners
Fax	May be personalised Record available	More time-consuming administratively than email May be distorted on arrival at location
First Class; Lotus Notes or other computer conferencing software	Efficient filing of all relevant work Ongoing discussion possible Threaded conversations will be recorded	Relies on partners going into the conference/bulletin board Initial setting up can have hiccups
Meeting between project manager and partner	Useful to resolve major problems and build on trust A strong indicator of both concern and support	Usually expensive, both in terms of travel costs and time

existing and potential funders, beneficiaries (past, present and potential) and the wider public, including private companies and the public sector. Naturally, the content of the dissemination activity will be varied to meet the needs and interests of the audience.

Activities may include:

- Leaflet – mailshots, inserts, and a handful wherever you go!
- Exhibitions – any products and one-page summaries of specific elements;
- Papers at conferences;
- Employment/careers fairs;
- Employer forums (project specific or as part of other events);
- Focus groups;
- In-company presentations;
- Linking with professional bodies;
- Journal articles;
- Local radio interviews;
- Websites;
- Audio cassettes;
- Video;
- CD ROM.

All partners need to demonstrate dissemination activities by the end of the project.

Evaluation and monitoring

A frequent weakness of many bids in the past is a failure to address how the project will be evaluated and monitored. This may be an entirely internal procedure (and will often be left to the project manager to initially implement), or payments for an external evaluator (sub-contracted from outside the partnership) may be built into the budget. There are arguments for both approaches, as well as drawbacks. One factor to bear in mind is that a good external evaluator, taking a formative approach, can support the learning and development processes of the project and help the partners spot any emerging difficulties before they become unmanageable. Both the project process and the products can be evaluated. Proposals should make it clear that partners are willing to participate in evaluation activities. The chapter on evaluation later in this book outlines the pros and cons of different approaches.

Budgets

As mentioned earlier, the financial elements of European grants are not always straightforward. The project budget should be distributed between all the partners. This may not be equally shared, as the partner responsible for project management may need more support than others. Salary levels and other areas of expenditure may be considerably lower in central and eastern Europe than in western Europe.

Major outlays in terms of actual cash from the project budget tend to be for travel to partner meetings, accommodation and subsistence. The project *Vademecum* will show the maximum daily rate that may be paid for different levels of personnel employed by the partner organisations to work on the project. Similarly, it will list maximum daily rates, varying between different countries, for accommodation and subsistence during partner meetings.

For many programmes, the required level of matched funding is around 50 per cent of the total budget. For most programmes, the letter of intent (see above) needs to specify the amount of the project grant that the partner expects to receive from the project, and what their matched funding contribution will be. The *Vademecum* states what resources and items of expenditure can be used as matched funding. Most organisations, apart from some private companies, tend not to fund in 'cash'; but instead offset staff time, equipment depreciation, room-hire, and other accepted items.

If at all possible, it is worth involving someone from the finance department, and better still someone with experience in European project finance, to help with the budget − both at the proposal stage and when completing the final report, which requires copious financial detail. Also, ensure that the financial budget relates to the project activities and milestones.

Avoiding predictable headaches

At almost any conference involving participants from the world of continuing education you will find a gaggle of people, huddled over their pints, bemoaning:

● The difficulties they have had in working with the [insert any EU nationality];
● Receiving information from the [insert any EU partner organisation] by the deadline;
● The unbelievable bureaucracy of those running the [insert any EU Programme];
● The delay in receiving information [eg contracts, funding, final payment] from the contractors or National Agencies.

Many of these difficulties result from unforeseen problems, but in my experience even in the proposal stage things can go horribly wrong.

The most common cause of despair comes from partners not getting information to the proposal writer on time, in particular, letters of intent. A faxed copy of the letter of intent will do (although the proposal writer needs to get a copy of the original letter in case this is ever requested by the Commission). It is easy to sit back smugly and point out that there is normally at least two months between the call for proposals and the deadline, not to mention the likelihood of learning informally when the next round of proposals will take place. So why the problems so late in the day? The underlying problem is that all partners need to approve the budget separately, and this takes time. Chief executives are always worried that they are somehow committing their organisation to something that might end up costing more than it brings in – and often, with EU programmes, this is exactly what happens. Little wonder, then, that chief executives delay signing the letter of intent until the last minute.

There can also be the disappointment of a partner dropping out at the last minute for whatever reason. In some cases this partner, or their type of organisation, or their country could be a deciding factor in its success. This may be one of those times when trusted contacts might know a good person to talk to. I have been in the position of telephoning organisations in Estonia a week before the deadline; whilst the first was politely interested, the second was exceedingly keen. Thanks to advances in office technology, the fact that she spoke good English, and had a genuine personal and organisational interest in the project content, all the information was exchanged in time, including receipt of the letter of intent.

As you progress through the proposal form there is often a sense of déjà vu, and a feeling that you are writing the same things two or three times. This may well be true. Many of the application forms do ask for the same information in different ways. Irritating though this can be, each question needs to be answered fully. Conversely, there are other parts of the application form where insufficient space is allocated and there is a constraint on the amount of information given; the best approach is to keep these sections punchy and elaborate elsewhere.

I am sure that those who have engaged in project proposal writing can regale a myriad of horror stories about writing proposals. It is simply not possible to prepare a proposal in the certainty that you can avoid all of the pitfalls. However, with sound planning, a belief in the actual content of the project, having a couple of trusted partners on board, and with the support of your organisation, it is possible to encounter only a few headaches along the way.

And finally...

Rather than a conclusion, let me finish with a few miscellaneous tips:

- Always use the word 'will' rather than 'would' when writing the application; ie make it appear that the project is real, rather than something that you are thinking about doing.
- Consider equal opportunities – how will your project show that it is offering 'equal opportunities'?
- Identify what is 'innovative' about your project; although what you are doing may not be something that is new and at the cutting edge, it may be that your approach has not previously been used in a different location; or

that combining complementary expertise with partners, you are doing something new.

- Refer to the project by its name when writing the proposal.
- Whilst you need to allow yourself the flexibility to deliver the project, make sure that the activities are clearly specified and appear logical to the reader; it is always possible to make minor changes once the project has started.
- Ask a colleague, or employ someone external to your organisation, to read your application; in particular, ask them to make sure that the proposal makes sense, that you have not made assumptions that the bid-evaluator will not comprehend, and that you have developed the bid logically.

Finally, don't forget to treat the whole exercise as a learning experience, and enjoy yourself!

References

Churchouse, C. and Churchouse, J. (1999) *Managing Projects,* Gower

Field, J. (1997) 'People networking' in Bell, C., Bowden, M. and Trott, A. *Implementing Flexible Learning,* Kogan Page, pp.171–9

Nuissl, E. (ed) (1999) *Adult Education and Learning in Europe: Evaluation of the Adult Education Action Within the SOCRATES Programme,* Deutches Institut für Erwachsenenbildung

Reiss, G. (1992) *Project Management Demystified,* E & FN Spon

3 Co-ordinating European lifelong learning projects: reflections on experience

Pamela Clayton

Background

Generally speaking, I work in the field of social exclusion, with particular reference to education/training and vocational guidance and counselling, and am based in a university adult and continuing education department. So far, I have worked as a team member on five projects and as co-ordinator and project initiator on two projects, all funded by the European Commission. To give an idea of the scope and outcomes of these projects, they have included:

- In 1994, a pilot research project, 'Vocational Guidance and Counselling for Women Returners', headed by CIRCE, a German research network. The outcomes were a report and a book (Chisholm 1997).
- In 1995, a pilot project, 'The Insertion of Young Graduate Women into the Labour Market', headed by INREP, a French training institute. The outcomes were a very innovative job-search method, a report (unpublished and only in French), and the insertion of a dozen long-term unemployed women with ethnic minority backgrounds into good-quality employment.
- 1996–9, a SOCRATES project, 'The Legal Status of Women in the European Union', co-ordinated by University of Paris 8, whose outcomes included a European module which in Scotland, was delivered to women recruited by a women's group and taught by a Community Development Worker (the module was ultimately incorporated into the law curricula of the participating universities); printed articles in English, French and Spanish (Azzoug and Demichel 1999); and a website.
- In 1996 I successfully bid for and co-ordinated a 2 year LEONARDO Survey and Analysis project, 'Access to Vocational Guidance for People at Risk of Social Exclusion' (Clayton 1999).
- In 1997 I became a partner on another 2 year LEONARDO Survey and Analysis project, 'Bridging the Gap; the role of vocational guidance in women's career development', led by University College Cork. The outcome will be a report.
- In 1998 I bid for funding for a 2 year LEONARDO pilot project using our previous research as the basis for an online training module (in Czech, English, Finnish and Italian), 'Access Issues in Vocational Guidance', for

guidance professionals and para-professionals. This is in progress (Clayton and Plant 2000).

- In 1999 I became a partner on an 18 month LEONARDO project, 'Immigrant Women and Vocational Qualifications', led by GATE, a German research institute in Hamburg, which will involve holding a conference in each partner country and a collection of case studies of immigrant women's prior (experiential) learning.

Overall, I have worked with partners from Denmark, Finland, France, Germany, Ireland, Italy, Luxembourg, Portugal, Spain and the Czech Republic; and, in addition, have prospective partners in Iceland, Norway, Sweden and Greece.

All of these have been learning processes in themselves, so what follows is an account of the lessons I have learnt, especially concerning the job of the promoter/co-ordinator. I want to say at the outset, though, that almost every-thing I know about both designing and running European projects I learnt by observing, and subsequently copying, my first project co-ordinator. I was very lucky to have such a good role model, rather than having to learn from others' mistakes – or my own (though I certainly do make mistakes to learn from). Whatever the qualities of the co-ordinator, though, I believe it is extremely helpful to be a project partner first. You need a bit of experience of multinational projects before taking on the multiple roles of the co-ordinator, which I explore in this paper: assembling partnerships; project design; funding applications; turning partnerships into teams; negotiation; handling difference; information management; dissemination and transfer; influencing policy-makers; getting support; handling problems; and a snapshot of the co-ordinator's life.

Putting together partnerships

When?

It is worth assembling the partnership well ahead of time

This allows the partners to have an input into the bid, and to develop a commitment to the project. It's also a good idea to start with more potential partners than you really need, as some will, for various reasons, drop out or prove to be inappropriate for that particular project.

Who?

There are three aspects to consider: the countries, the institutions and the indi-viduals. Partners may be chosen from the EU, the European Economic Area or the pre-accession countries. The countries involved should have a real interest, based on need, in the field.

The types of institution sought naturally depend on the nature of the project. Research projects may have rather different partners from pilot projects involving training. On another level, since the funding often takes time to arrive (and the final tranche may arrive long after the project is completed), partner organisations need to have sufficient reserves to survive in the meantime.

The type of individual, however, is another matter. For me, the important criteria are:

- Commitment to the aims and the ethos of the project;
- An ability and willingness to learn new skills;
- The proven ability to understand and speak English.

Previous experience, or even knowledge of the topic is not a requirement! (I had never heard of vocational guidance when I joined my first project – and the Finnish researcher on one of my projects knew very little about it on starting, but became so enthusiastic and knowledgeable that she became a guidance counsellor!)

The language issue is unfortunate, as it cuts out potentially valuable partners. Although I speak French and have been on two French-language projects, I find it too time-consuming to communicate in two languages and meetings progress too slowly, even with simultaneous translation by willing bilingual partners.

How does one find partners?

In my case, in a variety of ways:

- People I've worked with on other projects and whose work I've admired;
- People I've met or heard speak at conferences;
- Email correspondents who demonstrate interest and commitment;
- Personal recommendations from people whose judgment I trust;
- Recommendations by the national co-ordinating unit (NCU – in the UK this is the Department for Education and Skills, the DfES) or labour/ education ministry.

I (and anyone else) can now draw on a network covering every country in Europe, and many of mine are personal contacts – but this has taken years!

Designing the project

I have worked on two kinds of project: research and pilot projects. The latter consist of producing an outcome, such as a training course or software package; the former I'll say a little more about because it is a specialised form of research and is, above all, policy-oriented. Following the model of the first project I worked on, my research design consists broadly of qualitative and quantitative desk research, to find out what the existing situation is in each country on the given topic; case studies that demonstrate good practice; interviews with experts, the social partners (that is, employers and trade unions), policymakers and other interested bodies; analysis, conclusions and recommendations, applicable to each individual country and to all the European countries involved.

Should proposals be detailed or not?

My proposals tend to be very detailed, but this does not have to be the case. On the SOCRATES project the original conception was very vague: it appeared to consist only of a statement on the situation of women in France and the aim of producing and piloting a course. The gaps were filled in through discussion and negotiation at the transnational meetings, and the final outcomes were impressive.

Should all the partners have the same tasks or should they specialise?

My own projects have been of both kinds. In the 1996 project, all partners carried out the same tasks; but the 1998 online training module curriculum has been designed in Denmark; the distance learning elements suggested by the Glasgow University Distance Education Initiative (GUIDE); the original Report edited in Finland, Italy and the UK; additional data added by the Czech Republic; translation done in Finland, Italy and the Czech Republic; and piloting in the Czech Republic, Finland, Sweden, Italy, Greece, Scotland, England and Wales.

> **The important thing is that all partners make a concrete input and have a real role to play, even if those roles are different in kind or in amount of input**

Part of the point of such projects is to share knowledge and ideas, and take these forward.

Making the funding bid

I allow a 2 month period for this, and make a detailed timetable for all the tasks involved. Some important points are:

- Use the help available: full written guidance is given and National Agency personnel are very helpful.
- Cost the bid accurately and realistically, but add a percentage for inflation – remember that from doing your costing to starting the project will probably be 12 months, and till the end of the project a further year or more.

- Bid for money to translate products into all the partner languages, especially where the target audience is unlikely to speak the project language. Over-estimate rather than under-estimate the translation budget – it always seems, in my experience, to cost more than one thinks.
- Include letters of support from non-participating agencies, social partners and policy-makers.

European funding application forms tend to be tedious but easy to complete if you follow the rules. My costings tend to be very detailed, down to finding out the APEX fares for every partner to every destination and estimating the amount of photocopying paper I'll need! This hasn't prevented me making mistakes, but the Commission so far has been helpful when I've had to make revisions. It is possible to transfer up to 15 per cent between spending categories without re-negotiating the contract and this gives some leeway. In the 1996 project I was able to move money from the central travel budget (for transnational meetings) to translation.

Given that European funding is intended to have outcomes beyond the life of the project, it is both politic and genuinely useful to obtain letters of support, including people who will provide you with case studies, expert opinions, trainees, and so on.

Making a partnership into a team

In my view, an important part of the co-ordinator's role is helping the partners, who are not only from different countries but sometimes from different academic or professional backgrounds, to work as a team. This begins from the first transnational meeting.

- I try to set the tenor of the discussions by showing that I respect all opinions and ideas equally.
- We spend a lot of time together: we stay in the same hotel, take all our main meals together and generally talk non-stop for 12 hours a day!
- Shared linguistic competence in at least one language is helpful socially, as well as professionally.

My own projects have been mixed-sex, four of the others were all-women. In my experience this has had no relevance to the degree of bonding and co-operative working that has taken place.

An unexpected outcome of this kind of team-building arose when a promoter/co-ordinator left part way through, leaving a leadership vacuum. This was quickly filled by the partners from two of the countries working in concert, with the willing acquiescence of the others and the support of the lead partner's administrator, and the project was successfully completed.

Negotiating tasks

Where the original proposal is relatively open, negotiating the details is essential.

> **However even where the specification is already laid down and agreed, there is always scope for negotiation**

In the first project I co-ordinated, we developed further our methodology, with valuable input from the more theoretically-oriented Italian partners. We also had to negotiate the content. For example, there are few conventional guidance services in Ireland, but some unique initiatives, and little lifelong learning in Italy, but a lot of conceptual work on active and passive labour market measures.

Other matters for negotiation include:

- Deadlines – it's sometimes hard for the co-ordinator in her enthusiasm to remember that everyone is working on the project part-time within busy working lives;
- The format for presentation of materials.

In practice, I usually suggest a format and everyone agrees! (Though whether they follow it to the letter in the first instance is another matter...)

Handling difference

On the agenda of the first meeting of my projects is a discussion of:

- Our national differences, which we aim to explore and capitalise on;
- Our commonalities, including our shared ethos.

Working on social exclusion is in itself a bond and, unfortunately, social exclusion is widespread, rising and affects the same groups in all the countries I have worked with. I find it useful to include at least one partner from, for example, Italy, Spain or France, which have very theoretical academic traditions, along with the more pragmatic Irish and British. Since the former Eastern bloc countries are now eligible to join projects, I have developed valuable links with the Czech Republic, which, despite the problems of rapid and sometimes destructive change and financial difficulties, have much experience to share and initiatives to learn from.

Even where the project uses a single language, it's important to remember that partner who understands written English very well may have less experience with spoken English.

> **Linguistic competence varies, so all decisions taken at the meetings need to be written up in clear simple language and circulated as soon as possible**

Information management

This is a major task and email makes it harder, rather than easier. Filing (real and virtual) and record-keeping are the key. The following is based on bitter experience!

Email

- Devise conventions for the subject line (such as an acronym for the project and a short descriptive phrase), so that all partners know immediately which project the email is about and which aspect of the project is being addressed.
- Agree that all attachments should be in a common format, such as rich text format.
- Try to avoid sending too many emails – it can be confusing otherwise and we all receive emails from other sources too.
- File emails carefully in separate folders for each aspect of the project, for example, meeting arrangements, translated files and so on. Otherwise you will end up with hundreds of files in one folder and waste time every time you wish to refer to one.
- Keep a list, with dates, of all emails/file attachments sent and all emails/file attachments received (except for friendly greetings!), and send this list to partners each time you update it.
- If your emails are ignored, write, phone or fax – there may be a problem with the partner's email.

Accounts

Keep accounts as you go along or set aside one day a month for updating accounts. This is a horrible task when you are dealing with a number of currencies and have to turn everything into Euros. Where partners are in the eurozone, insist that they present any invoices in Euros. The rule is that the £/€ rate is that used when the money from Brussels is changed into pounds in your account. Make a note of this and keep it somewhere you can remember…

Timesheets

At the end of the project you and your partners will have to present a list of all the dates you worked on the project and the activities you performed. Again, this is best done as you go along. In practice, we probably work on several different projects on the same day, perhaps reacting to phone calls and emails. Just amalgamate the times – if you judge that you spend a total of 2 days' worth of work on a particular project in a particular week, choose two dates to assign to that project.

> **Keep on top of the filing and record-keeping and then it won't get on top of you**

Dissemination and transfer

This is high priority and a major task in itself – there is little point in projects which disappear from sight with nothing to show for them.

> **Ideally, all partners should disseminate the project findings in their own countries**

I begin at the bid stage by enlisting support, having explained the project aims, from relevant agencies, social partners and policymakers; tell them the result of the bid; involve them as case studies or expert interviewees; and inform them of the final findings.

In the case of my 1998 project, the report was available in print at cost and free electronically. I advertised the report on as many mailbases and list-servers as would accept it; had it put on as many websites as possible; took leaflets and a demonstration copy of the report to conferences and meetings; circulated information through networks; spoke about it at every opportunity (although a rather shy person, I am never shy at making my point whoever is there and however many people are present); encouraged feedback and engaged in dialogue with people who contacted me (whether to be critical or appreciative!); set up a mailbase for discussion (this was rather disappointing – people in the guidance world seem to be too busy for this); where possible, accepted all invitations to speak about the findings; published short articles in widely-read publications, such as *Adults Learning* and *News-check*; and provided case studies of the project to the NCU and others. The results of the dissemination strategy included the report being accessed from India, Hong Kong, Vietnam, Mexico, Russia, New Zealand, Australia, South Africa, Canada and the USA, as well as the UK and other European countries; and the other project partners and myself have been asked to speak in a number of forums.

There are several aspects to transferring project findings or products. Possibilities include:

- Mainstreaming, for example, a pilot course being adopted and recognised at local or national level, or taken up by another educational provider;
- Adoption in countries not in the original project;
- Turning research into pilot projects.

In the case of our 1996 research, we decided to transfer our findings through the present pilot module (unfortunately the Irish partner, who came up with this idea, was subsequently unable to join the new project). In this way, we hope to add to the amount of in-service training available to practitioners and, at the same time, highlight the existing good practice that we discovered.

Influencing policy-makers is extremely difficult – the hardest thing is to make contact, or even find out who the policy-makers are (in my experience, civil servants never admit to being policy-makers and politicians rush off before they can be asked leading questions). One tip is to include their support at the bid stage. For example, our supporters include the Equal Opportunities Commission (Scotland), the Scottish Trades Union Congress and the Confederation for British Industry (Scotland).

Projects often hold seminars at the end of the project to which are invited policy-makers, social partners, guidance workers, academics and relevant non-governmental organisations (NGOs). We were lucky in that one of the people who had evaluated our project bid brought along colleagues from the Scottish Office to our seminar. My DfEE (now the DfES) contact also arranged a seminar for policy-makers at which I was invited to speak about the problem our project addressed. A phone discussion with a Welsh guidance service led to an invitation by a Training and Enterprise Council (TEC) to deliver workshops. All these are small things, but one has to hope that they trickle down somehow!

Getting support

It is easy to feel very alone when problems arise, but quite unnecessary. There are two major sources of support:

- Your contact person at the National Agency and other colleagues there;
- Your contact person at the Commission.

For my first project I held the opening meeting in Brussels, so that I could meet my Commission contact, and I found it very helpful to have done so – it would have been a little harder to phone a total stranger. In addition, the National Agency seconds someone to the Commission to deal with all UK enquires. It was only when I met my DfEE contact that I realised the value of this support. Since then, I've met other people at the DfEE and the UK LEONARDO support unit, and can access help very easily.

There is no need to feel shy or that you're being a nuisance. Both the Commission and the National Agency want you to succeed – after all, you're spending their money! The National Agency also wants the prestige of national projects being funded and succeeding, not to mention the practical benefits. As mentioned before, I now consult the National Agency while preparing the bid – and under LEONARDO 2 this was to some extent routinised, since there were two stages: an outline bid to the National Agency and then, where accepted, a detailed bid.

Problems

The late arrival and relatively small amount of funding are annoyances (which makes it all the more important to have committed – and patient – partners). The accounting procedures are very detailed and take up a great amount of time, but what is worse, the project outcomes appear to be judged entirely by the Commission accountants, who neither understand nor care about the quality of your findings or product. Just be honest and transparent in your accounting, and swallow your irritation!

A different kind of problem arises where partners don't do what they're supposed to do. Where individuals have been carefully chosen, such problems usually arise from poor communication and can be sorted out with tact, patience and understanding. It would be useful to preserve some professional distance from project partners in case of conflict that cannot be resolved amicably – but this is difficult.

The co-ordinator's life

Face-to-face meetings are essential, notwithstanding the great benefits of rapid communication by email, fax and phone. Meetings not only allow negotiation of the process and content of the project, but also reinforce the common ethos and mutual respect that I think are essential for a good partnership. It is important to hold partner meetings in different countries. For example, there may be the chance to visit relevant projects, invite social partners to the meetings, meet the support staff with whom you'll often communicate – and, of course, to get a feel for the culture. The co-ordinator may visit each partner separately for what is called 'monitoring and evaluation' (but for me it's support, in-depth discussion and, where necessary, troubleshooting).

You may also be invited to attend seminars and conferences, at which you not only learn about new initiatives and other projects, but also have the chance to disseminate your own. Since I began my European project work, I've travelled from my base in Glasgow to Antwerp, Barcelona, Bergen, Brussels, Brescia, Copenhagen, Cork, Dortmund, Hamburg, Helsinki, Joensuu, Lleida, Milan, Paris, Oulu, Prague, Riga, Rome and Stuttgart (some of these more than once), not to mention Birmingham, Carmarthen, Edinburgh, Leicester, London, Manchester and Warwick. As co-ordinator, I like to arrive on Thursday afternoon; since meetings nearly always involve staying away over a Saturday night (in order to get economy fares), invaluable weekends catching up with domestic life are often taken away and I never make up the time. So the travel can be tiring and disruptive, and we work long hours during the meetings. Luckily, I do love visiting other countries, eating out and staying in hotels!

Aside from the travel, there is a huge amount of administration to do, involving time management, meticulous record-keeping and good communication skills. I do my own accounts and draw up contracts (with no relevant qualifications).

Don't even think about European projects if you're not prepared to travel and if you hate administration!

I have been lucky so far and have had no failed bids. If and when this happens, I shall contact my National Agency to find out what went wrong, in order to avoid making the same mistake. Certainly, and despite all, I intend to carry on bidding for European funding because of the transnational friendships I have made, the acquaintance with different academic cultures, the opportunity to travel, and the feeling that, in a small way, such projects can make a difference.

Conclusion

Co-ordinating European projects is a major task. Always time-consuming, it can also be frustrating, difficult and stressful. The time lag between bid and acceptance, between acceptance and receiving the money, and between putting in reports and receiving further monies make it essential that your organisation understands what European funding involves. There have already been improvements in the arrangements, with more responsibility being given to the National Agencies, and it is to be hoped that further streamlining will take place. The issue of late payment is a very serious one and makes it difficult for NGOs to participate, despite the expressed wish of the Commission that they will. The amount of record-keeping and information management require either a clear head or excellent secretarial support. Working with a collection of people from different language backgrounds takes care, even if you are working in only one language.

The compensations, on the other hand, are enormous: the opportunity to travel, to meet like-minded people from other parts of Europe, to share experiences, knowledge, approaches, and to produce something that you feel is worthwhile and might, in a small way, better the lot of fellow-Europeans.

Bibliography

Azzoug, M. and Demichel, F. (eds) (1999) *Le fil d'Ariane: The Legal Status of Women in the European Union*, Publication of the Institute of European Studies, University of Paris 8

Chisholm, L. (1997) *Getting In, Climbing Up and Breaking Through: Vocational Guidance and Counselling for Women Returners*, The Policy Press

Clayton, P. (1999) *Access to Vocational Guidance for People at Risk of Social Exclusion*, University of Glasgow, Department of Adult and Continuing Education and www.gla.ac.uk/Acad/AdultEd/Research/Leonardo.html

Clayton, P. and Plant, P. (2000) *Opening Doors: Social Exclusion, Adult Vocational Guidance and Access*, University of Glasgow, www.gla.ac.uk/avg

4 'The beautiful book': guidelines for producing transnational publications

Jenny Headlam-Wells and Carol Blackman

The context

This chapter arises from a European Social Fund project, 'WIM XXI: Women into Management in the 21st Century'. It was developed with funding from the Community Initiative EMPLOYMENT NOW, which sponsored a transnational network whose main aim was to encourage women's access to management positions.

Four European universities made up the network. In the UK, the University of Westminster, the University of Lincolnshire and Humberside and the University of Liverpool, and in Spain, the University of Valencia. The UK partners included a national charity, the 'Women Returners' Network', and the Spanish included the *Instituto de Economía Pública*. The network also included institutions and private centres of research and training: ISTUD (Instituto Studi Direzionali/Management Studies Institute) in Italy, BFI (Berufsförderungsinstitut/Professional Development Institute) in Austria and BFZ (Berufliche Fortbildungszentren der Bayrischen Arbeitsgeberverbände/Vocational Training Centres of the Bavarian Employers' Association) in Germany.

The UK project consisted of four major stages. Firstly, we carried out research with employers, women returners and managers to identify the barriers to women's progression to higher management levels, and the skills needed to overcome them. We examined the 'glass ceiling' in the UK and, through discussions with our European partners, compared it across Europe. Secondly, we used the research findings to design a management development programme for women wishing to return to work. Thirdly, we delivered six of the programmes at the three UK Universities, providing training for 80 women in all. Finally, we disseminated the findings to employer organisations, government departments, education and training institutions and other audiences. The work of the project over the 3 year period, 1997–2000, is discussed in detail in a transnational evaluation report (Universities of Lincolnshire & Humberside and Westminster 2000).

Transnationality

Transnationality was one of the guiding principles of the EMPLOYMENT and ADAPT Community Initiatives (EC 1999). For our project, the sharing of new and innovative ideas across national boundaries took a number of forms: the exchange of research findings in the early stages of the project; the design of training programmes for women wishing to reach senior levels in management; student visits from the UK to Austria and Spain; two international conferences; and a joint book produced by the UK and the Spanish partners.

The UK and Spanish projects produced a number of individual publications in their own language, which were in their original action plans (Mills *et al* 1998, Headlam-Wells and Mills 1999, Barbera *et al* 2000a,b). The joint book was not in our original action plan; rather it grew organically out of our close co-operation with partners at the University of Valencia. The UK and the Spanish projects had the most in common within the network, with close similarities in our research and training activities.

The two projects, however, targeted different groups of women. The UK project focused on the re-entry to the workplace of women whose professional career had been interrupted, usually for childcare reasons. The main aim of the Spanish project was the training of young women graduates with management aspirations. The biographical and professional profile of the students was therefore different, but the women were all university graduates and shared the same level of education.

Guidance on transnational publications

The working language of the network was English and the Transnational Report was written in English, with a contribution from each of the partners. However, for the book to be truly a joint work we wanted it to be published in both Spanish and English in a bi-lingual format. The result was: *Exceptional women: the career paths of women managers in Spain and the UK – Mujeres Directivas: promoción profesional en España y el Reino Unido*, published by the University of Valencia.

Co-coordinating a transnational publishing project of this kind is a complex process, and we certainly had our share of highs and lows in producing the book. With an ironic allusion to Spain's favourite sport of football, we got into the habit of calling our text 'the beautiful book'. As we have mentioned, the book evolved out of the project, rather than being planned at the beginning; this is the advice we would like to have had before we started:

- Start early, everything will take much longer than you think. We first had the idea for our book in April 1999 and we completed it in July 2000. The research and writing of our book took nine months; the rest of the time was needed for translating, rewriting, editing, production and distribution.

- Only attempt a bilingual publication when you have built up a good relationship with your partner. Schedule in as many face-to-face meetings as you can at an early stage and use them as deadlines for stages of the work.

- Use a common source of European statistics, such as the most up-to-date edition of the European Commission's annual publication, *Employment in Europe,* and make sure that definitions, for example of employment rates or unemployment levels, are mutually understood.

- With transnational research it is clearly important to describe the background of the countries in which the research took place, and to draw out comparisons and contrasts between the labour market contexts.

- Using the technology: all partners need to agree and have the same equipment and software, or equipment that is compatible. The most efficient means of exchanging documents is by email with attachments. However, be on guard for virus transfers.

- Get to the draft stage as soon as possible – get the words down on paper. Each country will need to produce its own draft first. The work to develop it into a joint publication starts from the point where you can compare and contrast the two drafts.

- Take a lot of care with the translation. The first stage is obviously to have a translation done by a mother tongue speaker. But the publication may need to be rewritten to match the terminology of the academic discipline in which the original contribution was written. This is very time consuming, but important if the book is to read as a continuous whole.

- In addition to using a translator, it is essential that at least one member of each partner team understands the language of the other country. There will be a number of ambiguities to resolve at short notice; these may need someone who knows the context of the project to advise on the most appropriate translation.

- Equip yourself with an advanced dictionary in the partner language at the beginning of the process. We wasted a lot of time with a basic dictionary that was inadequate for the subtleties of meaning that the text required, even after it had been professionally translated.

- Be sure that all partners are working on the definitive translation of the final copy – a lot of time can be wasted correcting draft versions.

- Appreciate the fact that different countries have different styles of writing. Our Spanish partners used far more words to express the same ideas: the English version of the book contains 129 pages, while the Spanish version runs to 145.

- If you plan to have a Foreword, leave plenty of time, particularly if you are approaching a government minister, as we did. The text must be available in its final draft form before such a person will agree to support it. Make your request at least 3 months before you need the Foreword, and allow at least a month once you have sent in the final draft. Include a summary of the project and of the key findings. Make it clear who is funding the project.

- Build in plenty of time for the production of the publication. We had not realised the amount of time that would be needed for the printing of our book. The University of Valencia subcontracted this out, and we and our partners had little control over the timescale. Time also needs to be allowed for the books/publications to be transported from one country to the other and then couriered from one UK partner to the other.

- Check the project completion dates with your prospective partner before you start. The UK completion date was 3 months earlier than our Spanish partner's and we were therefore under much greater pressure at the end. Leave plenty of time before the end of the project for sending out the publication – effective dissemination of outcomes is an important criterion of success for European Social Fund projects.

- Finally, be flexible, tolerant, and open-minded, and be prepared to compromise.

References

Barbera, E., Ramos, A. and Sarrio, M. (2000a) 'Género y organización laboral: intervenciónes y cambio', in J. Fernández (ed), *La intervención en los ámbitos de la sexología y la generología*, Pirámide

Barberá, E., Ramos, A. and Sarrió, M. (2000b) 'Mujeres directivas ante el tercer milenio: el proyecto NOWDI XXI', *Papeles del Psicólogo, (75)* pp.46–52

EC (1999) *Transnationality Works! If you work at it!,* European Commission

Headlam-Wells, J. and Mills, V. (1999) *Gender and Career Advancement: Successful Women Managers in the UK,* University of Lincolnshire & Humberside Research Paper, No. 32

Mills, V., Blackman, C., Headlam-Wells, J., *et al* (1998) *Through the Glass Ceiling: Women in Management,* University of Westminster Research Report

Sarrio, M., Headlam-Wells, J., Ramos, A., *et al* (2000) *Exceptional Women: the Career Paths of Women Managers in Spain and the UK,* University of Valencia Press

Universities of Lincolnshire & Humberside and Westminster (2000) *WIM XXI Women in Management in the 21st Century – Transnational Evaluation Report of 1997–2000 Partnership,* Universities of Lincolnshire & Humberside and Westminster

5   Networking and intercultural communication: triumphs and tribulations

Lore Arthur

Britons work harder, Greeks smoke and Finns are suicidal, announced one newspaper headline (*The Independent*, 15 October 1999). According to the reported European Union (EU) survey, the Germans spend the most on medical care, the Austrians on entertainment and culture, and the Irish by far the most on education, books and newspapers, while the Britons have the largest ownership of video recorders. It is not my intention to interpret these findings. Instead I aim to point to cultural differences in ways of understanding and doing things that persist and multiply in an increasingly homogenising global world. The perceived differences are reflected in talk of 'foreigners' or 'going abroad', not only in a negative but also in an enriching sense.

Different circumstances provoke different reflections, attitudes and moods in an indefinable way. When abroad, the experience of being a 'stranger' or 'foreigner' is, for many, a route to self-discovery. Previously held sets of belief and behaviour accepted as the norm in the home country may be challenged by other people's points of view and conventions. Similar tensions are found within Europe, where regional identification seems to be increasing, yet, at the same time, more than 63 per cent are proud of their country and nationality. Extremely proud, according to EU statistics, are the Irish (92 per cent), the Greeks (91 per cent) and British (81 per cent). Predictably, the Germans are an exceptional case; here only 45 per cent are proud of their nationality (EC 1995).

However, we not only identify with our country or regional community, but also with the community of adult educators. In adult continuing education, or in vocational education and training, or any other form of education, we collaborate with European partners within one of the many EU-supported programmes, and take part in international conferences or numerous professional networks across Europe.

Networks and partnerships

International networking between adult educators is not a new phenomenon. The World Association for Adult Education was established in 1918–1919. Following the Second World War there were several UNESCO world conferences. The last one, CONFINTEA, was held in Hamburg in 1996. The European Association for the Education of Adults (before 1998, the European Bureau for Adult Education), with a membership of 120 organisations in 28 countries, or the Council of Europe, founded in 1949 with the aim of promoting reconciliation between the states and peoples of Europe, have been active networking bodies over many years. ESREA, the European Society for Research in the Education of Adults, was founded as late as 1991 and now has over 350 members who are linked to a lively email network. Other networks provide information, including the ALICE Network (Adult Learning Information Centre Europe), which has up-to-date information on informal adult education in member countries. The many EU-supported action programmes, such as ERASMUS, LEONARDO or LINGUA, all integrated into the SOCRATES framework in 1995, have proven to be successful, at least in terms of intercultural collaboration. All of these projects point to a considerable number of people who have experienced, or are currently experiencing, interactions with people from other countries who speak different languages and come from different cultural backgrounds.

Then there is the computer. By the year 2010, it is estimated that 80 per cent of UK households will be connected to the internet (*Independent*, 20 December 1999). The phenomenal growth in CMC (computer-mediated communication) has captured both popular and scholarly information. Cultural theorists and technophiles have been quick to envisage sweeping changes in the social order. The potential of CMC to bring people together, for better or worse, has practical consequences both for individuals and for social order. It is not unreasonable to expect that virtual communities, like communities in real life, are there to protect the interests of their members. CMC systems are believed to have powerful effects on social relations, particularly since they are perceived to be egalitarian and democratic – which may, in reality, not be the case (Herring 1996).

Networking is also a social activity. Coleman (1994) introduced the term 'social capital' to describe individuals making the best use of their own resources in the context of social relationships, such as family, community, even professional organisations. Network theorists often refer to two broad concepts of network models: the pluralist, voluntary, non-hierarchical one and the corporatist one, which is non-competitive, hierarchical and functional (Marsh and Rhodes 1992, 13). Most professional networks, particularly those in adult and continuing education, tend to be pluralist, egalitarian and self-determined in their conception and organisation, with the leadership responsible to its members and with apparently easy communication processes. When joining a network, and this may sound too obvious, it may be worthwhile to clarify issues such as decision-making processes and confidentiality.

In the international context, particularly in networks involving members of a number of countries who do not all share the same mother tongue, fundamental barriers of communication can occur. One of the main aims of the SOCRATES projects on adult education (1995–1997) was to enhance the perception of European cultures, and to encourage an exchange and to improve mutual acceptance among them. The final report of MOPED (Monitoring as a Process of Dialogue) concerns the evaluation of all 102 adult education projects. The report describes how members of the various projects dealt with language problems: how project partners agreed on a working language and how they adapted themselves to that language. The variety of languages was felt to be enriching, but also lessened the efficiency. Reciprocal explanations of terminology were considered necessary, which were time-consuming and difficult to realise. More than one language itself, and the differences in cultural background, proved to be a problem – though sometimes, the report notes, partners of a monolingual were equally confronted with divergent ideas (Nuissl 1998).

In Europe there remain distinctive academic and organisational traditions. Furthermore, adult education has developed in different ways in the north and south of Europe as well as the east and west. Intercultural variations, it seems, merit further clarification if deep-level understanding is to be achieved.

Interpreting cultural meaning

Within the EU there is to be a flowering of cultures, respect for cultural and linguistic diversity and, at the same time, a striving for a common cultural heritage (CEC 1992). Yet concepts of a shared cultural heritage with other European countries remain elusive and difficult to grasp, let alone usable as an instrument for learning in the intended spirit of the Treaty. The understanding of anything 'European' remains full of contradictions and dichotomies. More often than not, we are more aware of the differences between us, in terms of languages and cultures, than of the similarities. Not surprisingly, paradigms of culture, even intercultural communication, pose a multitude of questions, yet offer few answers.

Even the word 'culture' differs in the English language from the dominant European convention that equates it with the idea of 'civilisation', aesthetic achievements and individual performance. Within the Anglo-Saxon context, the concept of culture has been understood in a far more pluralistic sense and applied, until relatively recently, on a far more sparing basis (Jenks 1993). Raymond Williams considers culture to be one the most complicated words in the English language. 'This is partly because of its intricate historical development, in several European languages, but mainly because it has now come to be used for important concepts in several distinct intellectual disciplines and in several distinct and incompatible systems of thought' (1988).

The richness and diversity of European cultures at local, regional and national level pose their own barriers, tension and challenges. There is an assumption that almost everybody on the Continent speaks fluent English, and in the professional context this may well be true. However, the dominant language spoken by one in four people, or 25 per cent of the EU's population, is German. The second most frequently cited mother tongues are French, Italian and English, each spoken by 16 per cent of the European population. Spanish is spoken by 9 per cent and Dutch by 6 per cent, while the remaining languages do not exceed 5 per cent. One in three EU citizens on the other hand, speaks English sufficiently well to take part in conversations, and if English mother tongue speakers are included, this figure rises to one in two (EC 1996).

Altogether there are almost 50 indigenous languages, spoken throughout the EU (European Bureau for Lesser Used Languages 1998). Admittedly, even linguists have difficulties in clarifying what constitutes a language, as opposed to a dialect. Furthermore, languages as well as dialects convey not only geographical, but also social information about their speakers. The notion of a dialect refers to a distinctive grammar, vocabulary range and pronunciation.

The most common problem relates to mutual intelligibility. A language has been defined as 'a dialect with an army and a navy', but there are serious undercurrents to such a statement. In the words of Fairclough (1998),

> modern armies and navies are the features of the nation state, and so too is the linguistic unification or standardisation of large politically defined territories which make talk of English or French meaningful. When people talk about 'English' in Britain, for instance, they generally have in mind British standard English.

The decision, therefore, about what constitutes a language is made on grounds of history, economics, politics, and usually, though not always, in relation to national boundaries.

The English language has, in the minds of many people, become the world language by virtue of the political progress made by the English-speaking nations in the past 200 years or so, and it is likely to remain so, rapidly consolidating its position across the world. It is estimated that 350 million people have English as a mother tongue, and a further 400 million use English as a second language with official status in over 60 countries. Estimates also indicate that at least 150 million people use English fluently as a foreign language, and three or four times that number have some degree of competence (Crystal 1994). One cannot really blame the British people for their lack of linguistic skills. Which language are they to learn? It is not surprising that in the UK the ability to speak another language has rarely achieved the educational or social status it deserves – much to the detriment of the many bilingual or multilingual speakers resident in the country. But there are warning lights ahead: 'Native speakers of English may feel that the language 'belongs' to them, but it will be those who speak English as a second or foreign language who will determine its world future' (Nuffield Languages Inquiry 2000, p.15).

In Europe, the languages situation is driven by two seemingly contradictory tendencies. We can express these in terms of massification and diversification, both of which are in operation simultaneously (Clyne 1995). Examples of massification are open economic borders between member states and the homogenising effect of the English language, coupled with Anglo-American culture, not only in Europe but also across the globe. On the other hand, diversification is exemplified in the resurgence of regions in western Europe and the re-emergence of smaller, largely language-based nation states in central and eastern Europe.

However, in Europe there are also the languages spoken by migrants. London, for example, was recently described as the most multilingual capital of the world, with some 250 to 300 languages. One might argue that, as the consequence of socio-economically or politically driven processes of immigration, the traditional pattern of language variations across Europe have been considerably extended over the past decades. It is assumed that in the year 2000 one-third of the population under the age of 35 in urban Europe had an immigrant background (Extra and Verhoefen 1993). The largest numbers are noted in France and Germany, with 8 and 6 per cent respectively, though reliable data continue to be difficult to collect. As migration increases and monocultural states become less common, cultural identity becomes more complex, less tied to geographical locations, less static and more individualised.

In practical terms, this means that when in contact with colleagues from other countries one should not assume that they represent that country or that culture. Nor should one assume that the necessity to speak English is either always welcome or easily achieved. Furthermore, the inability to understand the other language can be a grave handicap. In the European institutions, for example,

> the most effective members by far are those who can speak or understand several languages – very few Brits amongst them and even when translation and interpreting services are available at official meetings, it's in the corridors, cafeterias and members' offices that the real business is done, the compromises are reached and the amendments are drawn up. (Nuffield Languages Inquiry 2000, p.17)

Furthermore, 'Yes, other people use English because it is practical to do so – but they do not expect to have to use it all the time in their own country, within and outside working hours' (Nuffield Languages Inquiry 2000, p.20).

How is one to cope with another language when time is simply not available to study it over many months? It is more than just a truism to state that the British are often considered to be linguistically illiterate. They are just not expected to be able to speak French, German or Spanish. This can be an advantage, to be exploited for practical purposes. For example, even when one does not speak the other language it would be advisable to acquire a few words.

- When giving a presentation it is useful to say a few opening phrases in the target language, even if the remaining text is given in English. Colleagues from other countries tend to really appreciate such an effort, particularly since it is not expected.

For those who do have some skills in the other language the following lesson from experience is worth considering:

- It is worth concentrating on developing listening skills. It is surprising how far one can get with a few words in the other language, provided one can guess the gist of what has been said in response. Furthermore, it is easier to understand answers to 'closed' rather than 'open' questions!
- Professional or technical language rarely causes problems since there usually is enough common ground between all speakers and the language of business tends to be English. Instead, the 'off duty' social language is important when people like to talk about, for example, the latest political scandal, cultural events, football results and family relationships, rather than work.

'National characteristics'

Terms such as national characteristics or national style are often controversial. They carry with them meanings attached to monocultural societies, which are no longer valid in the contemporary context. It may be difficult to argue that individuals are typically German or English. However, the notion that people from different countries and cultures have distinct characteristics is still widely accepted in organisational and management theory. In everyday reality, too, particularly in commerce and industry, the understanding of what may be termed national style or national characteristics is part of numerous acculturation training programmes. Before they are dismissed entirely, therefore, it may be useful to look at what is being discussed. For example, it is generally accepted in industry, and a source of much research, that power relationships, patterns of organisation and communication processes vary from one culture or country to another.

Laurent (1983) investigated national differences in the perception of what management should be in nine European countries and the USA. National culture, he argues, seems to act as a strong determinant of managerial ideology

– something which adult education cannot entirely ignore when in touch with organisations from other countries. In his research, Laurent found the Germans to be less hierarchy conscious than the British, which may surprise many people. On the other hand, more Germans, in common with Belgians, French and Italians, expected their managers to be 'the expert', that is, to have precise answers on hand to most questions subordinates might ask, unlike their Swedish, British, Dutch or American counterparts. There are important consequences for those who are supporting adult learning. For example, the role of the 'expert' is also widely accepted in adult education circles in many continental countries.

Hofstede (1980, 1991, 1998), perhaps the best known exponent of cultural differences in organisations, regards concepts of culture as forms of collective programming of the mind. He links personality to the individual, and to collective national, regional, social class and organisational cultures. His large scale survey findings address issues such as how frequently employees are afraid to express disagreement with their managers, or subordinates' preferences about bosses' decision-making styles. Hofstede identified differences in thinking and social action over a wide range of occupations in multi-national companies in 40 nations (later increased to 50). He eventually positioned these countries into four, largely independent indices:

- Power distance (unequal versus equal);
- Uncertainty avoidance (rigid versus flexible);
- Individualism/collectivism (alone versus together);
- Masculinity/femininity (tough versus tender).

These values are attributed to various countries. For example, those sampled in Britain and Germany shared equally low positions in power distance indices, which are based on employees' fear of disagreeing with their superiors. Germans score very much higher than their British counterparts in uncertainty avoidance, showing a need for security and dependence. In other words, in many German organisations (including those of adult education), decisions are rarely made speedily at the middle level of management – unlike in Britain, where middle managers generally have more freedom of action. With regard to what Hofstede calls masculinity and femininity, Britain scored relatively high in the former, higher than France or Spain but less high than Japan, Austria or Switzerland, while Sweden, Norway and other Nordic countries, perhaps predictably, scored high in the latter. These terms refer to, for example, job-centredness, emphasis on visible achievements, competition, decisiveness efficiency on the one hand and, on the other, employee-centredness, centrality of personal and family life, human relationships, co-operation and solidarity.

If useful at times, such approaches are also open to questions. Clyne (1994) refers to difficulties that have arisen from German unification and which demonstrate a much more pronounced sense of collectivity and uncertainty avoidance in former East Germany when compared to the West. The playing down of nation states and general political changes in Europe is arguably not an altogether suitable basis for describing cultural variations. Other factors, such as class, gender and age interrelate with aspects of individualism and collectivity. They challenge our perception and understanding of long adhered to ways of seeing the world.

- When negotiating agreements it is important to establish clear decision-making processes and responsibilities. Professional titles rarely serve to clarify the situation. Furthermore, the time factor in reaching decisions can be frustrating to British colleagues, who are not familiar with other systems.
- When writing letters or sending emails it is worth finding out who in the other office reads such messages. It is customary in many German institutions, for example, for all members of staff to read all incoming and outgoing communications, which may not always be appropriate.

Intercultural communication

The relationship between so-called national characteristics, language and thought is a complex one. To see them as three points in a constantly flowing continuum is surely more accurate than, for example, to see them as an isosceles triangle, with one dominating the other two (Valdes 1986). Most of us, however, think of language as a means of communication with two or more speakers in social context and social interaction. The word 'communication' derives from the Latin equivalent of common (*communis*), and denotes an interaction between the sender and receiver of messages, who exchange thoughts, ideas and experiences in specific locations or periods of time. There is an assumption that they have something in common. However, both sender and receiver generally adhere to culturally determined and accepted conventions in their own language. For example, most people in any kind of business or personal interaction know how to address each other, when and how to interrupt, how to maintain the dialogue, or seek clarification.

In normal circumstances we have strategies on hand if the flow of a conversation stops, or if we have not understood something. The matter becomes more complex if the speaker tries to communicate in a language other than his or her own. It is surprising how awkward and insecure a tongue-tied person can suddenly feel. It is not uncommon to feel like an outsider when conversations are not in English, or when they are in English but are filled with jargon or technical language. Miscommunications occur regularly and in almost any kind of social setting, even in the first language. It is not surprising that the need for increased cultural understanding and improved intercultural communication has become increasingly important in a world of blending cultures, experiences and professional practices. In the words of Lambo (1975),

> Individuals, groups, departments of knowledge, peoples separated by culture differences, failing to make themselves understood across barriers of prejudice, suspicion, and misunderstanding of motive, live in dangerous tension. Even in dealing with highly technical matters, professionally trained men and women encounter obstacles constructed of prejudices and emotional attitudes that impede their joint effort.

This statement may be a quarter of a century old, but it would be difficult to deny its validity – even in the contemporary context.

Culture-specific ways of speaking can provoke misunderstanding, even prejudice. The French, for example, tend to make requests using the future tense, imperatives and *il faut*, thereby conveying the impression of authoritarianism, impatience and assertiveness. Germans, in common with Greeks, use fewer *downgraders* (please, sort of, I suppose) than their English-speaking colleagues. Instead they use *upgraders* (absolutely, I am sure, you must understand), which, to English ears, makes them sound assertive if not aggressive. Spaniards consider constant interruptions a form of polite interest in the topic on hand, conventions again not readily accepted in the English-speaking world (or at least, not in Britain).

Even academic discourse, both in written and spoken form, may also vary. Clyne (1995, p.138) in his discussion on communication patterns, describes how in the German education system, as in many other countries across the world, essay-writing is far less important than in English-speaking countries, where assessed written assignments are a major part of the curriculum. In German-language countries they are largely language exercises and the formal rules are far less important. Furthermore, in many continental countries, *content* is paramount in expository discourse, rather than the structure of the *argument*. English-speaking scholars, when writing, tend to use advance organisers to make the text more predictable. The less linear and less formal structure of content-oriented academic discourse is evident in books and academic articles, as well as in oral presentations – and digressions are often misunderstood as transgressions.

- British humour, though admired world-wide, is not always as funny as it seems. For example, most Greeks, in common with many other nationalities, generally require thoroughness in presentations, which they expect to contain a wide range of statistics and facts. They want to be informed, rather than amused.

- It is worth noting that most continentals use language in a more direct manner. Even if they seem to speak what seems to be perfect English, they find it difficult to cope with nuances, inferences, word plays and phrases such as: *You couldn't possibly...?* instead of the more direct *Can you...?*

Other factors influence cross-cultural understanding, such as posture, movement, the stretching of hands, bowing or facial expressions, gaze eye movement, gestures and physical distance, all of which have a particular role to play in effective communication. It is surprising how seemingly trivial matters such as when to use first names, when or when not to shake hands, or even kiss in the manner of the French, can cause confusion and a sense of insecurity.

Conclusion

It is not my intention to state the obvious, or present what may seem platitudes. Anyone used to a multicultural environment will already be sensitised to many of these issues. On the other hand, there are subtle power relationships to be considered. It is surprising how de-powered and insecure one can feel when in situations where the language of communication or the environment is not familiar.

There are, however, more positive aspects to be considered. No matter how complex cultural and linguistic differences may appear, in the reality of everyday life those involved in education and training share many similar concerns. These can revolve around issues such as financial resources, staffing and organisational management, even teaching methods and a concern for equal opportunities and equal chances, irrespective of the national or regional constraints with which they are confronted, or the type of organisation to which they are committed. There are shared values and experiences that bond relationships in a professional context, just as a love of football, food or the arts helps to bond social ones.

In international relations there are no hard and fast rules, or reliable books full of tips on dos and don'ts, which might help ease communication. Such lists of tips would seem endless, anecdotal and superficial. Yet they relate to cultural awareness and to language and, at the same time, to similarities and differences in dealing with colleagues from other countries, in terms of organisations, structures and policies, which would help to avoid potential pitfalls. It may be reassuring to think that customs and conventions vanish in most societies, not only within a given time span, but also across countries and localities as national boundaries become less important. However, new ones emerge. Thank goodness. There is much pleasure to be found in cultural richness and diversity. As the French say, '*vivre la différence*'! – hopefully for many years to come.

References

Coleman, J.S. (1994) *Foundations of Social Theory.*, The Belknapp Press of Harvard University Press

CEC (1992) *Treaty on European Union,* Office for Official Publications of the European Communities, Commission of the European Communities

Clyne, M. (1995) *German Language in Changing Europe,* Cambridge University Press

Clyne, M. (1994) *Intercultural Communication at Work. Cultural Values in Discourse,* Cambridge University Press

Crystal, D. (1994) *An Encyclopaedic Dictionary of Language and Languages,* Penguin Books

EC (1995) *Eurobarometer 42,* European Commission

EC (1996) *Eurobarometer 44,* European Commission

European Bureau for Lesser Used Languages (1998) *Mini Guide to Lesser Used Languages of the European Union,* European Bureau for Lesser Used Languages

Extra, G. and Verhoefen L. (eds) (1993) *Immigrant Languages in Europe,* Multilingual Matters

Fairclough, N. (1998) *Language and Power,* Longman

Herring, S. (ed) (1996) *Computer-Mediated Communication. Linguistic, Social and Cross-Cultural Perspectives,* John Benjamins Publishing

Hofstede and Associates (1998) *Masculinity and Feminity. The Taboo Dimension of National Cultures,* Sage Publications

Hofstede, G. (1991) *Cultures and Organizations: Software of the Mind,* McGraw-Hill

Hofstede, G. (1980) *Culture's Consequences. International Differences in Work-Related Values,* Sage Publications

Jenks, C. (1993) *Culture. Key ideas.* Routledge

Lambo, T.A. (1975) *Getting the Message Across: An Inquiry into the Successes and Failures of Cross-Cultural Communication in the Contemporary World,* The Unesco Press

Laurent, A. (1983) 'The cultural diversity of western conception of management' in *International Studies of Management and Organisation,* XIII:(1–2), 75

Marsh, D. and Rhodes, R.A.W. (eds) (1992) *Policy Networks in British Government,* Clarendon Press

Nuffield Languages Inquiry (2000) *Languages: The Next Generation,* The Nuffield Foundation

Nuissl, E. (1998) *Adult Education and Learning in Europe. Evaluation of the Adult Education Action within the SOCRATES Programme,* DIE

Valdes, J. (ed) (1986) *Culture Bound,* Cambridge University Press

Williams, R. (1988) *Key Words. A Vocabulary of Culture and Society,* Fontana Press

6 European partnerships: exhilaration or exasperation?

Mike Osborne, Martin Cloonan and Iddo Oberski

Introduction

In this chapter we consider lessons arising from our experience of three European collaborative projects. Each of these projects, involving the Institute of Education at the University of Stirling, demonstrates a range of issues that pertain to networking on a pan-European scale. We have focused on what we believe to be the major challenges of such projects, with the aim of assisting others in making a balanced and well-justified decision regarding their own participation in European projects.

The three projects are as follows:

- Thematic Network in University Continuing Education (THENUCE), funded within the Thematic Network strand of the SOCRATES programme, involving some 80 universities across Europe and co-ordinated by the European Universities Continuing Education Network (EUCEN) (described below by Mike Osborne).
- Performance Indicators of Quality Assessment in Higher Education, a TEMPUS project, co-ordinated by the University of Economics in Bratislava, Slovakia (described below by Martin Cloonan).
- European Learning in Smaller Companies (ELISC), a LEONARDO Strand II.1.1 project, co-ordinated by the University of Stirling (described below by Iddo Oberski).

THENUCE

The aims of this project were firstly to examine the European dimension of university continuing education and secondly to identify cross-disciplinary and administrative issues of common interest for co-operation. EUCEN proposed this project under the Thematic Networks strand of the SOCRATES Programme. The project findings were intended to have a lasting and widespread impact on the development and management of CE programmes, and could thus be regarded as a key instrument for the enhancement of academic quality in this area.

THENUCE was funded at 36 per cent of total cost (€100,000, out of a total cost of €275,000), for the academic year 1996/97, the remaining

64 per cent being supported by the participating universities. The project was then renewed for the two following years, at a similar level of budget, lasting until 1999. At the core of the Thematic Network was a European Scientific Committee. This was a large and inclusive group, consisting of one national expert from each of the 18 participating countries, together representatives of the associated National Network partners of EUCEN (such as UACE, in the case of the UK), the CRE (Association of European Universities), of Switzerland, of Central European partners and of the SOCRATES Technical Assistance Office.

In the first year, each national expert produced a National Report of good practices and obstacles/problems in university continuing education in their own country. These were then consolidated into a European Report (Soeiro 1997), targeted at a high level readership that included the European Commission, Rectors/Presidents of universities, national/regional government agencies and other decision makers.

During the second year, tools were developed to disseminate good practices and identify possible solutions to enhance the development of university continuing education on a European level. Fourteen working groups were established, each consisting of between five and eight active members. Each group worked on a specific and agreed topic, such as: the role of academics in university continuing education (CE); the training of university managers of CE; research in the learning process; cost–benefit analysis in university CE; accreditation and quality; and co-operation with networks (THENUCE 2000).

The third year was dedicated to disseminating new knowledge on the introduction of flexible ways of acquiring and accrediting of skills. Six major dissemination activities were undertaken:

(1) *THENUCE Managers Handbook* (Mitchell 1999);
(2) THENUCE observation project, with an aim to create linked national level observatories;
(3) THENUCE seminar project, with a focus on working collaboratively with the CRE whose 40th anniversary conference in Bordeaux was centred on lifelong learning;
(4) THENUCE dissemination project, with the 'horizontal' aim of connecting most sectoral studies and actions started during the initial two years work of the project, and to ensure maximum visibility of this work;
(5) THENUCE IT/multimedia whose CD-ROM demonstrates innovative uses of communications, information technology and multimedia in UCE (Osborne *et al* 1999);
(6) The THENUCE conference in Reykjavik, which saw the final dissemination for the entire project (THENUCE 2000).

Reflections and observations

From the perspective of one of those involved as a national expert in the first year, working group co-ordinator in the second year and task group co-ordinator in the third year, there are a number of issues that can be described by an insider.

Resourcing networks

At every level, the establishment of such a network requires a vast amount of 'in-kind' contribution. Indeed, the financial model adopted by the European Commission assumes this, and recognises 'in kind' contributions for the purposes of match funding. There is little prospect that those involved in such networks will benefit financially, and therefore those taking part need to reflect from the outset what they and their organisation may gain from involvement. My observations suggest that in an area such as university CE, which is broad ranging as a field across Europe, perceived benefits are extremely varied, and include; the opportunity to network; to develop better ways of managing and administering programmes; to explore new pedagogical possibilities; to add value to development by exploring research dimensions; and to simply have a good time. For most participants, THENUCE has provided all of these.

Establishing networks

It is quite clear that to establish networks of credibility from the outset, access to a pre-existing pan-European network is vital. This was the case for THENUCE, which grew out of the existing membership of EUCEN. Even then, such networks require highly organised administrators, rapidly responsive members and good links with other agencies, particularly within the Commission. THENUCE was extremely successful at continuing to engage its members, and sustained an active membership of between 50 and 80 institutions over the period of the project. This level of activity was only feasible because the network was built upon a well-established organisation, which then overtly used its existing organisational base as a platform for expansion geographically (particularly into eastern Europe), and as a means of developing inter-agency co-operation (with other thematic networks, and with CRE in particular).

Sustaining networks

To maintain a network that inevitably has all the dynamics of any large group is a daunting task. Predictably, there were tensions at times within THENUCE. Communication is a major issue so, of course, the advent of rapid electronic communications systems was of great assistance. The use of web pages and mail-servers became routine, and members were frequently consulted electronically, as well as through regular meetings. Even so, a number of executive decisions inevitably had to be made in order to steer the project as a whole, and to ensure that individual working groups and task forces achieved their goals.

Communication also can be difficult at times because of language. As in many European networks, English was the chosen common language. This clearly limited the participation of some colleagues and led to an over-representation of those from the UK. This was particularly problematic in such a field as university involvement in CE, where there is a far more long-standing tradition in the UK than in most other European countries.

An import element of continuing success was continuing networking with other agencies. THENUCE was particularly successful in this way. For example, THENUCE was defined as a 'horizontal' network, with significance for all parts of the university system, in contrast with the 'vertical' networks, which were each based in a single discipline. As one of two horizontal networks (together with one other in open and distance education); THENUCE was considered to be concerned with a field of endeavour (albeit an under-developed one) that touched upon the interests of all specific discipline areas (the 'vertical' networks). It was therefore agreed that it would be desirable to establish co-operation with some of the other networks and, indeed, THENUCE hosted a forum of some 28 other thematic projects in Dublin in October 1997. Links with the CRE, and particularly collaboration with the organisation of their 1999 conference on lifelong learning, have also been very important. Many other examples of such links can be quoted and these clearly have created a good impression within the Commission.

In conclusion

In 1999, at the end of 3 years, a substantial output of material was achieved. The final output included 18 national reports and a comparative analysis of the situations in each of the countries considered (Soeiro 1997), other publications, both in print and electronic form, and a number of dissemination events. To quote Soeiro:

> the major asset of the European Report, based on the contents of the National Reports and from the active contribution of all partners, is that it can provide a possible basis for a future strategy on UCE in Europe, enhancing the importance of the national inputs. The idea is that from what is being done in UCE in the participating countries the best practices may be disseminated bringing the European dimension a greater richness and diversity, taking advantage of the fact that widening the selected exchange of information in the field of UCE will certainly improve its quality.

This is, perhaps, an optimistic assessment, since there is considerable variability in the various reports, but there is no doubt that much of potential transferability has been achieved. Furthermore, a well-established group of collaborating individuals and institutions now exists, and their numbers were swelled when more universities joined a fourth year, THENUCE-DIS, which aimed to further disseminate the work of the 3 years. Plans were in place for further 3 year network bids, THENUCE+, which was aimed to give greater focus to work in Central and Eastern Europe, and ODELUCE, which aimed to link open and distance education more closely with university CE. This suggests that, despite its size and complexity, THENUCE has had a number of beneficial results, not only for EUCEN and its member institutions, but also for the visibility and credibility of university CE within the European higher education (HE) policy community, as well as within the Commission itself.

Performance indicators of quality assessment in HE

The aim of this project was to assess ways of using performance indicators as a means of ensuring quality within HE. More particularly, it aimed to incorporate best practice into the Slovak HE system, by building on the experiences of the European Union (EU) universities.

In 1996 three Slovak Universities – the Economics University of Bratislava; the University of Matej Bel, Banská Bystrica; and the University of Safarik, Presov – applied for funding under the Commission's TEMPUS programme (which was created to assist the reconstruction of the former Soviet states of eastern Europe). These programmes depend on the support of EU-based project partners. In this case, the foreign partners were the Universities of Hull (UK) and of Limerick (Ireland), the Hogeschool van Arnhem en Nijmegen (Netherlands), the UK's Quality Assurance Agency (QAA), and the University of Stirling. The bid was successful and yielded a grant of €151,580 for 2 years, from January 1998 to December 1999.

Following an initial meeting of project co-ordinators in April 1998, representatives from the three Slovak universities visited Stirling in August 1998 to familiarise themselves with the University's methods of quality assurance (both internal and external), as well as the national (Scotland and UK) systems. The visit included discussions with heads of departments, a pro-vice chancellor, senior administrators, and the Secretary of the Scottish Higher Education Funding Council (SHEFC). From these meetings a picture emerged both of the Scottish (and UK) method of assessing teaching and research, and of general issues concerning quality audits and the use of performance indicators (PIs). In the following 15 months there were more team meetings, conferences in Slovakia and further visits to UK institutions by the Slovak universities. The final project meeting was in December 1999.

As a representative of the University of Stirling I made two trips to Slovakia (for a team meeting and a conference) and organised two visits to Stirling for Slovak staff. There were several meetings and conferences at which the University of Stirling was not represented, but many members of staff at Stirling gave freely of their time when Slovak staff visited. One of the additional benefits of these visits was that it gave me the chance to meet staff in different departments at my own institution. For me, this included liaison with members of the University's senior management team in ways that many researchers never experience.

Observations

Although much more could be said about this project, I would like to make the following general observations.

The real costs

Superficially, European projects cover their own costs. In practice, many of the costs are not met, and this means that institutional goodwill has to be mobilised. The terms of the funding for this project gave an annual total of €2,000 to partner institutions, on the basis of 200 hours of secretarial work at a rate of €10 per hour. Travel expenses and a fixed daily rate covering accommodation costs were paid for staff travelling to Slovakia. However, this level of funding did not cover the staff costs to my institution. While European projects often require in-kind matched funding from the partner institutions, on a strictly commercial basis the University would have been out of pocket. Thus, a certain amount of international goodwill is being relied upon to facilitate TEMPUS projects. Although this is understandable, it might mean that only certain (eg junior, temporary) staff are released to perform this work. This could mean that the long-term benefits of participation in these projects (such as networks, further funding application) are less likely to materialise.

Partnership

Senior Slovak academics justifiably expected to meet senior UK academics as part of the project. While this was comparatively easy to arrange for meetings within the UK, getting senior members of the university to travel to Slovakia was not easy, partly because senior staff tend to have full working schedules and partly due to lack of funding for staff time, as described above, with all travel having to include a Saturday night to obtain low-cost air fares, and local travel to Bratislava via Vienna being hampered by border crossings.

Communication

Project meetings were conducted in English and presented few problems. Conferences were in Slovak with simultaneous translation into English for non-Slovaks. However, between meetings most communication was by fax, which often took the form of requests for action at short notice. This was the cause of some frustration. Email contact tended to be too sporadic to be reliable. Cultural differences also made themselves felt. There is more deference to status within Slovak institutions than within UK institutions, and this sometimes had the effect of making working arrangements over-formal by UK standards.

Research

This project had the potential to produce some research, primarily in the form of case studies about introducing PI systems in the partner countries. Research outcomes, in the form of published articles in academic and professional journals, would have given additional value to and justification for participation in the project, in particular for UK departments with their colleagues' beady eyes fixed on the Research Assessment Exercise. But to do such research justice, detailed knowledge of the Slovak system would have been required, and this would have entailed collaborative work, in addition to study visits and conferences. Although there is still the potential for this, the project has formally come to an end and this opportunity may have been missed. Although research is usually not the main motivation behind TEMPUS projects, it is likely that many have research potential that remains unfulfilled. Perhaps UK partners should explicitly negotiate joint papers for publication in refereed journals as a prerequisite of involvement.

Summary

This was an enjoyable project to work on, but its overall impact remains unclear and will only emerge as and when Slovak universities change the way quality is assessed and assured. At a personal level, the project provided the chance to gain insights into the problems of a newly emerging education system, and to visit a variety of places within Slovakia. My hosts were always generous, while remaining somewhat formal by UK standards. The downside of the project was the frustration caused by sometimes unrealistic expectations on behalf of Slovak colleagues and by the ultimately unrealised potential of parts of the project. In sum, I would recommend partnerships with eastern European colleagues, but only by going in with eyes open, being patient and keeping a strict eye on the *real* costs and benefits of involvement.

ELISC

The three main objectives of ELISC were to:

- Translate, contextualise and develop for internet delivery the Certificate in small- and medium-sized enterprises (SME) management, developed by the University of Stirling, in the partner countries Finland, Italy and Spain;
- Evaluate a pilot delivery of the Certificate in each partner country;

• Develop an accreditation framework that will allow transfer of learners and recognition of credit across the partner countries.

ELISC was a 3 year project, running between 1998 and 2000. It was co-ordinated by the University of Stirling, where it developed out of an earlier UK project on learning in small companies, which was funded by the DfEE (Seagraves *et al* 1996).

ELISC achieved some significant outcomes (Oberski *et al* 1999). However, there were delays in the Commission administration at the time the project was approved, and some of the initially projected developments and impacts could not be achieved at the envisaged level. Perhaps the project therefore lost some of its innovative nature. Despite these limitations, significant progress was made on developing and piloting the SME management course in three of the four participating countries, and plans for commercialisation of the web-delivered course were underway as the project ended.

Observations

Costing the proposal

There are some difficult tensions to resolve when estimating costs for a new proposal. ELISC was allocated €209,000 from the Commission for a total estimated project cost of €304,572. Halfway into the project two of the four main partners had already 'spent' their in-kind contribution (staff time) so that the total estimated cost of the project was €342,493, reducing the Commission's contribution to the project from 69 per cent to 61 per cent and increasing the cost to the partner institutions. A rule of thumb used in the physical sciences when calculating large-scale European projects is that one full-time staff member is required to realise project targets for every £30,000 of funding. If this had been applied to ELISC, then 7.5 full time staff would have been needed for the duration of the project and the in-kind contribution (their salaries) would be even greater.

This poses a difficult challenge. On the one hand, it is important to budget realistically at the project proposal stage to ensure that in-kind contributions are accurately represented, but on the other hand competition for funding effectively drives down the cost of projects (on paper, but not in reality). It may be that ELISC was particularly costly, as a result of the translation and contextualisation of course material, and the subsequent development for web delivery in each of the partner countries.

Financial administration

The requirements for financial administration of LEONARDO projects are set out in a Handbook. Any questions can be addressed to the national agency or the EC's LEONARDO offices. It is wise not to under-estimate the demands on both time and knowledge required for efficient running of the project finances. The Commission strongly recommends that the financial aspects of the project are not also carried out by the project co-ordinator and I agree with this. It would be best, in the case of a university, to use the existing expertise within finance departments to administer this aspect of all European projects, rather than have the project co-ordinator of each European project also take care of the finances.

In ELISC we ended up considering sub-contracting the financial management, to free up the co-ordinator's time for progressing project objectives more intensively. Within financial administration, we found it helpful to see the project as a separate entity entirely, so that travel, subsistence and other costs were initially charged to the institution and then, by the institution, to the project according to the regulation of eligible costs and approved daily rates, rather than direct to the project.

Partnership – formal and informal

We found that it paid – literally – to be flexible about who was and was not formally a member of the ELISC partnership. The initial partnership consisted of around 30 organisations. These comprised six educational institutions and training organisations, one external evaluator, a chamber of commerce, a Local Enterprise Company (LEC – the equivalent of a Training and Enterprise Council in England and Wales) and 21 SMEs. The project proposal was first submitted to the Commission in 1995, revised for 1996 and finally approved in 1997. By the time approval had come through, most of the SMEs that had initially shown an interest could no longer sustain involvement. Inevitably, given that they operate in a dynamic environment, some of the small firms had undergone significant changes, such as down-sizing, new ownership, changes in strategy, or changes in interest. Two educational institutions also no longer wished to be involved. Some new companies were recruited to the partnership and by 2000, ELISC consisted of four educational institutions, the external evaluator (EUCEN), a LEC and four SMEs.

While ten SMEs were actually involved in the project, most were not official partners. We chose to work with SMEs in this way to reduce the administrative costs of withdrawing and adding partners to the project. A partner in the project must, by the Commission's regulations, both receive funding from the project and contribute in kind and, therefore, each partner receives a contract from the promoting organisation (University of Stirling in this case). If a partner wishes to withdraw, the Commission requires a letter stating this, and the amount of funding received. Similarly, if a partner wants to join, a letter of intent needs to be received and a contract issued. All these documents then are sent to the Commission for approval. Although these procedures seem quite straight-forward, obtaining documents from partners that were no longer involved proved particularly challenging. By allowing SMEs to participate, for example, by piloting the course material for free, in return for staff time and feedback, both formal and informal partners still receive the benefits of working together, without the administrative hassle and cost (for example, one of our UK SMEs informed us that it costs them £100 to raise an invoice).

Partnership co-ordination and maintenance

Probably the most important aspect of establishing and maintaining a partnership is reaching a shared purpose, agreed objectives, a willingness to work together and, above all, the capacity to communicate.

At the start of ELISC a special FirstClass server was set up at the University of Stirling. All partners were given the client software and access to the server. It was then possible for every partner to get in touch easily with every other partner, and to keep up with project progress. Synchronous on-line chat was used for weekly meetings with partners to discuss progress and courses of action. We believe that FirstClass was instrumental in establishing the partnership and without such a tool it might have been difficult to progress the project quickly and at short notice.

Working with colleagues across Europe is a very rewarding experience from a personal perspective. There are opportunities to travel and be introduced to another culture in a personal way, rather than as a tourist, being made to feel at home wherever one may visit. Obviously, certain barriers need to be overcome and it may sometimes be difficult to communicate in a second or third language. Repeated clarifications, questioning, checking understanding and a good sense of humour all help in this process. It is tempting to attribute the lack of progress, or lack of communication, to a partners' cultural or national affiliation but, objectively speaking, I have not encountered any significant problems with our transnational partners that might not also have occurred with colleagues nationally, or within the same institution.

Finally, staffing issues are closely associated with the strength and stability of the partnership. The initial applicants to a project are often senior members of staff who, after a project has been approved for funding, may delegate the management and co-ordination to more junior staff. This may then impact on the partnership in two ways, senior staff may be perceived to have lost their commitment to the project, thereby possibly demotivating the partners, while junior staff may be more likely to move on to other posts, unsettling the established links, threatening continuity and reducing the long-term benefits. In ELISC, local co-ordination in each of the partner countries was transferred from senior management to temporary staff early on in the project and, at the time of writing, three of these have moved on elsewhere.

Conclusions

From our reflections on these three European projects we have arrived at the following points. These should help to ensure the successful operation of EU-funded projects.

- Define clearly the role of each organisation and individual within the project. Explicit agreements should be established about responsibilities and executive powers, both within and between organisations.
- Clarify again how the objectives of the project relate to the institution's objectives, as soon as the project is approved. There can be a considerable time gap between application and approval, so that priorities within organisations, as well as roles of individuals, may have changed significantly by the time approval is gained. Only become involved (especially as a promoter) if the project matches existing strategies within the department. For example, if research is a priority, then development projects are unlikely to fit the agenda.
- Calculate the real cost of the project, both operational and in terms of staff time. This should also include some consideration of the cost of missing out on other opportunities as a result of participation in the project (opportunity cost).
- Ensure the availability and involvement of both senior and permanent members of staff, in order to establish continuity and credibility. This, in turn, requires a realistic estimate of workload (administration, travelling, communication, dissemination, finance, and so on) and efficient human resource management.
- Examine how the organisation's existing financial management structures (in terms of both people and systems) will support a smooth running of the project's budget, in line with EU guidelines (for example, what happens to exchange rates, bank charges, international payments?) and establish clear responsibilities and protocols in this area, both within each organisation and between the partners.
- Never give up! We submitted the ELISC proposal on three separate occasions before it was successful, taking account of feedback and of our own evolving thinking.

References

Mitchell, V. (ed) (1999) *THENUCE Managers Handbook*, EUCEN

Osborne, M. *et al* (1999) *Innovative Uses of ICT and Multimedia in UCE*, EUCEN

Oberski, I., Osborne, M., Noya, C. *et al* (1999) 'European Learning in Smaller Companies', *Continuing Professional Development* 2 (4)
    www.openhouse.org.uk/virtual-university-press/cpd/welcome.htm

Seagraves, L., Osborne, M., Neal, P. *et al* (1996) *Learning in Smaller Companies Final Report*, University of Stirling

Soeiro, A. (ed) (1997) *Interim Report 1 – European Report Socrates Programme Thematic Network Project on University Continuing Education* 26-203-CP-1-96-1-BE-ERASMUS-ETN www.fe.up.pt/nuce/EUROPEAN.html

THENUCE (2000) *Thematic Network Project in University Continuing Education* www.fe.up.pt/nuce

7 Adult education and social purpose: the work of the International League for Social Commitment in Adult Education, 1984–1994

Vida Mohorčič Špolar and John Payne

> Our grave concern over the social inequality and social injustice which exist in nations throughout the world, coupled with our firm belief in adult education as a powerful force for social change, have led us to create the International League for Social Commitment in Adult Education, an organisation dedicated to social equality, social justice, and collective and individual human rights. (Preamble to the purposes of ILSCAE, agreed at the 1984 conference) (ILSCAE 1987)

Introduction: Europe and the world

There are at least four ways of understanding the concept 'Europe'. First is the geographical view of Europe, as a land mass stretching from the Atlantic to the Urals and from Scandinavia to the Bosphorus. Second, is the narrow, but important, institutional view, which sees Europe as synonymous with the European Union (EU) and its projects, which aims to reach a new settlement between the international (USA-led) neo-liberal economic project and the western European social-democratic model. The third views Europe as a conglomeration of political entities and states, which includes member states of the EU, aspirant members, particularly among the ex-command economy states of central and eastern Europe, and those countries, such as Norway and Switzerland, which are attempting to find a separate way forward. Fourth is the concept of Europe as a set of states at various stages of economic and social development, with varying relations to one another, but all existing in the context of a global neo-liberal economy that involves the movement of capital, people and culture and profound space–time dislocations of traditional societies (Castells 1998, 5). This fourth definition is most relevant here.

The International League for Social Commitment in Adult Education (ILSCAE) was a brief but significant attempt to re-interpret social purpose adult education from a global perspective. It both built on successful traditions of local social purpose adult education (eg Highlander in the USA;

community development in Latin America; mass literacy campaigns; trade union education; folk high schools) and attempted to develop an understanding of the links that bind localised activity together. It recognised, as did the global Jubilee 2000 debt-relief campaign, with its symbol of the chain, that links are at the same time links of oppression (binding people to oppressive social and economic systems) and of emancipation and solidarity (the peoples of the world linking arms).

It was an enormous task, and unsurprisingly ended in failure. Or rather, it has yet to succeed; we are aware of various current attempts to re-establish the organisation. However, part of the purpose of this piece of writing, a joint effort between the last two secretaries of the international co-ordinating committee, is to define the space that ILSCAE occupied and which is still available for adult educators wishing to promote international understanding and solidarity. One unintended outcome already has been to revive interest in the possibility of re-establishing ILSCAE in some new form. Using e-mail, opinions were sought from a number of people who had been active in ILSCAE over the years. Many of the views expressed in this paper are theirs, as well as our own. We hope, therefore, that even before publication, this particular writing project may have achieved some purpose.

ILSCAE – purposes

The objectives of ILSCAE were set out at an early date and remained substantially unchanged, although the practices resulting did change. Hal Beder remembers that another USA member, Tom Valentine, sat up all night during the originating conference at Rutgers University (1984) to write the charter. This was agreed at the final town meeting of that conference.[1] Subsequently (either in Canada 1988 or in Nicaragua 1989) a number of amendments were made to clarify the objectives (including the omission of the first objective) and these changes are shown in italics in the table below.

Purposes and practices

In gathering material for the present text, we focused on these purposes, and what, in the context of these purposes, the strengths, weaknesses and personal

---

[1]The town meeting concept was adapted from the practice of the early colonies in North America. Every member of a community could attend, every member had a voice. This democratic form is still retained in some small communities in the USA. However, as we shall see later in this text, the sense of common purpose, and the ability to listen to other points of view, were both problematic within ILSCAE.

The purposes of ILSCAE

Original version **(ILSCAE 1987)**	*Revised version* **(ILSCAE 1993 leaflet)**
1. To encourage all those involved in adult education to foster participation in dialogue on the critical social issues confronting humankind today, such as class inequality, environmental concerns, peace, racism, sexism and ageism	1. To encourage all those involved in adult education to identify and act to overcome the social, political and economic forces which perpetuate the existence of poverty, oppression and political powerlessness
2. To encourage all those involved in adult education to identify and act to overcome the social, political and economic forces which perpetuate the existence of poverty, oppression and political powerlessness	2. To encourage all those *involved* in adult education to view and practice adult education as a vehicle to enable all adults to gain and exert control over their own lives *as part of the community and the environment*
3. To encourage all those in adult education to view and practice adult education as a vehicle to enable all adults to gain and exert control over their own lives	3. To encourage all those involved in adult education to *direct resources towards the exploited, the* oppressed and politically powerless *and to work in solidarity in developing* learning activities *with* social, political, economic, cultural and aesthetic content
4. To encourage all those involved in adult education to work with the poor, oppressed, and politically powerless in learning activities which have social, political, economic, cultural and aesthetic import	4. To encourage *adult educators to learn about oppression from the oppressed, to name their own oppression, and to make explicit the ethics and values which guide their practice*
5. To encourage all adult educators to make explicit the ethics and values that guide their practice	5. To encourage [...] the preparation of adult educators to provide not only for the enhancement of technical skills, but also for the critical examination of ethical and social issues
6. To encourage those responsible for the preparation of adult educators to provide not only for the enhancement of technical skills, but also for the critical examination of ethical and social issues	6. To encourage the design, conduct and reporting of research and other forms of scholarship focusing adult education as a force for social change.
7. To encourage the design, conduct and reporting of research and other forms of scholarship focusing adult education as a force for social change.	

Commentary

- The dropping of (old) objective 1 from the original Charter is curious, given that, in practice, these issues have provided the content for the majority of presentations and activities at ILSCAE conferences.
- 'control over their own lives *as part of the community and the environment*' in new objective 2 emphasises the rejection of a view of empowerment stemming from humanistic psychology as free-floating, and somehow independent of social context.
- The revised objective 3 opened the way to solidarity work in parallel with movements linking struggles in the South with progressive social forces in the North.
- The strengthening of the ethical statement (new objective 4) had important practical implications in encouraging conferences which engaged with local struggles and issues in the host country, something identified below as ILSCAE's main contribution to the organising of international conferences.

significance of ILSCAE had been for these people.[1] One striking point about responses (from the UK, Germany, Sweden, Latin America and North America) was that no-one could find a purpose they disagreed with. For most respondents, objective 1 (our numbering refers to the revised objectives), with its clear statement about poverty, oppression and political powerlessness, sums up ILSCAE and leads on to the other purposes. However, one person also stressed the fourth (learning about oppression from the oppressed) and it was a particular feature of conferences from 1987 onwards that increasing emphasis was placed on visiting local projects and initiatives, rather than the reading of academic papers. This, in turn, caused difficulties for members with full-time academic jobs, for whom such activities were a core justification of the time and resources they were using for ILSCAE business. One respondent related this to his view that that research issues (purpose six) had been little developed, which again had had professional significance for him:

> I agree with all the aims. However, I found that when the research aim was neglected the organisation no longer served the scholarly require-ments of my position as a professor of adult education.

Another correspondent felt that the aims may have been too ambitious:

> I still support the aims and am pursuing them in my own way. But I think our practice in ILSCAE did not, and perhaps could not, match the grand ambitions of the aims because we were all institutionally and individually part of the 'forces of oppression'. This is not a criticism so much as a sociological observation. The members of ILSCAE had reputations, jobs, mortgages and other material factors at stake. I think we never really grasped the magnitude of the gap between us in the West and the 'oppressed' in the Majority World, or even between home-owning professionals and unemployed people living on run-down (public

---

[1]See Appendix 1 for the pro forma questions.

housing) estates. Really meeting these aims involves life challenges which are greater than most of us are honestly willing to accept.

A Latin American respondent, in declining to send in detailed comments, said that she had never felt she knew what the organisation was all about (*'la verdadera problemática de la organización'*). After two conferences she still felt that she had not got 'inside' the problems and successes of ILSCAE (*'no llegué a interiorizar los problemas y los éxitos de ILSCAE'*).

Unique features of ILSCAE

ILSCAE conferences implicitly criticised standard international adult education conferences from a number of directions:

- Most international conferences are not international because they have limited (if any) representation of people and issues from the south;
- People who attend international conferences tend to be professionals with secure state or academic jobs, with little representation from grass-roots educators;
- Most international conferences ignore the context in which they happen – the problems and achievements of local adult educators and learners;
- There is too much weight placed on content, too little on process and communications.

In ILSCAE, there was a heavy stress in the early conferences on process, on what one European member from the early period described as 'the tyranny of dominant languages, … the reconciliation of competing truths, and the co-existence of differently expressed endorsements of (the) purposes (of ILSCAE).' This is very apparent in the report of the 1986 conference (ILSCAE 1987) which is unlike a conventional academic conference 'proceedings' in containing considerable material on the issues (eg gender, literacy and language) and processes that had dominated the conference.

Throughout ILSCAE's lifespan, there was a strong criticism of the view that questions about adult education are purely technical or procedural in nature, a view most strongly expressed by the Canadian, Michael Collins:

> Critical practice calls for direct engagement in definable concrete projects for social change without which talk of justice, emancipation and equality become hollow rhetoric. (Collins 1991, 119)[1]

One respondent linked the unique features of ILSCAE explicitly to the aims, especially 'before such topics became stronger on the national and international levels.' As ILSCAE developed (particularly from the Netherlands

---

[1]See also Newman 1994 and Welton 1995.

conference of 1987)[1] the actual location of the conference became increasingly important:

> The unique feature of ILSCAE included primarily a conference which explored social change resources and the nature of specific local struggles where the conference was being held.

In the context of the long drawn-out low-level war in the North of Ireland, the 1992 Derry conference was especially important, with visits to a wide range of adult education and community development projects, and workers from those projects invited into the conference to discuss the views delegates had formed of their work.

The subjective elements of adult education as social commitment were important too. Another respondent described

> a (shared) sense that all was not right with the world and that adult education should incorporate some form of commitment to social change. And this ... was the network's strength – it allowed us an opportunity to discuss our work ... within a wider social analysis of the forces generating inequality and social exclusion.

In a similar way, another person came to see herself as 'part of an international educational movement.' In a published version of her views on ILSCAE, she suggested that, in order to make 'a contribution to struggles for social justice':

> The work of adult educators has to move beyond isolated pockets and classes to becoming a dimension of the work of wider social movements – working class, women's, disabled, environmental. (Barr 1999, 45)

For two grassroots inner city adult education workers, ILSCAE provided a rare opportunity to attend conferences and be part of international networks, because of the way it emphasised sharing of experience, and encouraged the involvement of practitioners. Like other respondents, they contrasted the space provided by ILSCAE with the normal work situation:

> We feel that it was especially relevant to adult basic education workers, and that in (our country) we are not encouraged to acknowledge or explore our own political motivation or to work politically in an up-front or direct way. ILSCAE was both a good forum in which to explore the politics of education and a safe place in which to express our own political views.

---

[1]See Appendix 2 for the dates and locations of conferences, and the names of the host organisations.

There was also implied criticism of the narrow, technical nature of much of the education and training of adult education workers, which largely ignores issues of social context and purpose:

> When I started working with ILSCAE I was naïve but I am naïve no longer. I learned a great deal about the world, my country in the world and international politics. These are among the most important lessons I ever learned and work with ILSCAE profoundly affected my life.
>
> The unique features of ILSCAE were the way it brought together adult educators round a cluster of values and purposes from a diverse range of organisations and types of work, rather than the more obvious institutional links ... For me personally there were a number of conversations and contacts which were important but the main thing was the encouragement and ideas I got which could be applied in my own locally-based work.

Problems, problems, problems

Potentially, ILSCAE was a powerful, international, grassroots-led non-governmental organisation (NGO). The reasons why it did not develop into such an organisation, with a secure place in global lifelong learning networks, were all too apparent in reference by respondents to the problems of ILSCAE. Those mentioned centred on organisational capacity, conflicts of interest and personal conflicts, and political views. These will now be considered in turn.

Organisational capacity

ILSCAE never had an organisational base with even minimal facilities, such as an office and staff. It relied entirely on the goodwill of organisations for whom its officers worked. Its main resource was time, telephone, postage 'borrowed' from larger organisations (the word 'steal' did occur in the title of one ILSCAE conference presentation!). In turn, this supposed the existence of people in positions of authority who were willing and able to 'turn a blind eye' to what was going on. Additional resources were sometimes forthcoming and were used to make it possible for individual people from the countries of the south, or from less well funded projects in the north, to attend conferences. However, aims and achievements diverged: following the success of Swedish adult educators in raising considerable funds for the 1985 conference, the 1986 conference report noted a fund-raising target of US$15,000 per year, against only £840 actually raised (ILSCAE 1987, 14). Only four of 19 presentations at Toronto (1988) were from the south, while 19 out of 22 proposed presentations by people unable to attend were from the south (ILSCAE 1989, Appendix 1).

Conflicts of interest and personal conflicts

Even in the north, there were obvious differences between people with tenured academic posts, who were able to attend conferences in working time, and find at least partial support for travel and fees through their organisation, and those working part-time, or for NGOs and other grassroots educational projects, who often ended up spending their own time and money on ILSCAE conferences. Thus, there were different levels of commitment involved for different people in becoming active in ILSCAE. As one respondent pointed out, this was exacerbated by the presence at early conferences of USA graduate students receiving 'credit' for conference attendance, although this might be more positively viewed as awakening the students' awareness by gently pushing them to think more critically about the social commitment tradition within adult education. The editorial group who produced the report of the 1986 conference in Nottingham, UK (all London-based practitioners) noted, for example:

> We have given people's academic qualifications where they have been given by contributors. As an editorial group, we feel that the system of academic qualifications is oppressive, though The League itself has not taken a position on this issue. (ILSCAE 1987, 5)

ILSCAE always led an uneasy existence between the conflicting demands and interest of academics, advocates and practitioners.

The objectives of ILSCAE speak of oppression. Personal experience of such oppression (based on gender, ethnicity, class, disability) varied between ILSCAE delegates. This led to impatience and animosity, with people only too willing to speak out about oppression (theirs and/or other people's) but less willing to listen to those with different understandings. William Dowling, a USA member, expressed it like this:

> All of us need to learn from each other. ILSCAE can provide a forum for that learning, but not if significant portions of the membership are alienated by behaviour that does not tolerate divergent views, or, worse yet, actively puts down with ill-concealed scorn the evolving concepts and ideas being developed by those whose learning about some of the issues is at a more beginning level. (ILSCAE 1989, 79)

Yet this kind of democratic tolerance often seemed at a premium within ILSCAE. A European member recollected that 'a small group of members seemed not to be interested in learning from others at all, which was sad.' And there is no doubt that the difficulty experienced by ILSCAE in dealing with issues of tolerance and oppression in personal and interpersonal relations had consequences for the League itself. Such issues must be resolved if there is to be a future for ILSCAE or any organisation with similar aims and working methods. Turning away from ILSCAE did not mean turning away from the values and aims that had attracted people in the first place: 'Why spend time in a destructive environment when there is much to do in the world that really is in the direction of ILSCAE's objectives?'

Political views

There was a strong sense in the early years that the organisation was dominated by North Americans (its founding conference had been at an American university) at a time when the USA government under President Reagan was pursuing an aggressive foreign policy, especially in central America. However, most North American members saw themselves as 'liberals', a term that has different connotations in different parts of the world. In the USA this meant that they were identified as potentially dangerous and subversive elements, challenging many of the mainstream values of the American government. But in Europe, and in particular the UK, 'liberals' were seen as weak, ineffective people who failed to analyse situations in terms of power as expressed through race, class and gender. Europeans in ILSCAE tended to identify themselves as 'radical' or 'socialist' or 'feminist' or some combination of the three terms. One USA respondent identified the Bergen (Netherlands) conference in 1987 as the one at which splits became open and irreconcilable:

> Things changed dramatically in Bergen. There were lots of divisions over liberal/radical positions, South Africa, university/non-university and just plain interpersonal animosity. (...) One problem was that given different cultures and different conflict resolution styles we never did establish norms and structures that enabled us to work together towards common goals. The forums and town meetings just could not handle it. Another problem was that after divisions started, everything became highly charged politically and even minor issues became major ones. Finally, although ILSCAE had a clear purpose, the meaning of democratic social change varied substantially among us.

One respondent claimed that 'some academics from North America' boycotted the next conference in Toronto (1988) and, indeed, the report of that conference shows a remarkably low participation by North Americans and reflects accurately a divided and confused organisation (ILSCAE 1989). Holding a conference in Nicaragua in 1989, at a time of open conflict between the US government and the Sandinista government, was not designed to heal the, by then apparent, rifts. However, for the few North Americans who did go to Nicaragua, that experience has remained with them ('in my mind and heart', as one person put it).

Adult education? Yes but...

There is an implicit assumption at most adult education gatherings that all work that goes under the heading of adult education is of value. To be an adult educator is to be on the side of 'good'. We believe ILSCAE challenged that assumption, and this is best represented for us in the report of the 1994 conference. This was held in the idyllic alpine setting of Lake Bled in Slovenia, not far from the killing fields of Bosnia. Each section of the conference report (Gender issues; 'Race', ethnicity, refugees and nationalism; Economic power and citizenship; Civil society and voluntary organisations) began with the same words:

> Most adult education does not change society. It confirms the powerful in their positions of power (people with more initial education get more adult education and training) and it confirms the powerless in their position (they are often unable to take part because of barriers of money, access and a sense that 'education is not for people like us'). But ... (ILSCAE 1996)

The 'But ...' was followed by a series of questions that reflected the many ways in which adult education begins to challenge the status quo in society, and can help people begin to shift the weight of oppression bearing upon them. It is a rather more modest view of adult education than that in the ILSCAE charter, but one that allows for the role of adult educators as agents of change, for the wide variety of contexts in which we operate, the problems we face, and our own understanding of what words like 'oppression' and 'liberation' mean.

ILSCAE's inability to break away from the 'conference mould' meant that its work centred on annual, highly charged conferences, rather than more modest projects and ways of exchanging ideas and showing solidarity. Except in the first 3 years, newsletters were never produced on more than an intermittent basis, proposals to develop international interest groups petered out, and detailed proposals for solidarity work in Nicaragua after the 1989 conference did not bear fruit. However, individual members made a contribution through their work in the south (for example in Chile, Mexico, Palestine) while, as we indicated above, individual friendships flourished, practice was inspired and horizons expanded by international contacts. ILSCAE did not change the world, but its members were changed by ILSCAE.

A future for ILSCAE?

Eventually the organisational problems lead to ILSCAE's demise (or rather inactivity, because ILSCAE still exists on paper). The British members, who came to dominate ILSCAE from an organisational aspect post-1989, had nothing like the access to 'borrowed resources' of colleagues in North America or other European countries. A number were directly affected by the break-up of the Inner London Education Authority in 1990, which forced them to seek employment in more poorly funded organisations with weaker resource bases. An attempt to set up a secretariat in central America was a failure.

Any person(s) or organisation(s) seeking to breathe new life into ILSCAE or a similar organisation must take account of four facts:

- The existence of a distinctive model of conference relevant to practitioners and advocates of lifelong learning, but also relevant to those academics who see adult education theory as fundamentally a 'theory of practice', set in economic, social and political contexts, rather than the prevailing technical – rational model.
- The uniqueness of ILSCAE: no respondent in our survey was able to identify an international organisation that is taking forward the purposes of ILSCAE.
- The likelihood that any attempt at resurrection will fail unless it can provide a firm organisational base, and make creative use of the different work contexts, political views and educational emphases, which exist among those who identify their work as 'a vehicle to enable all adults to gain and exert control over their own lives as part of the community and the environment'.
- The extent to which English, although an international language, still excludes many people from international events. Translation and interpreting, as we found on numerous occasions, are expensive and imperfect ways of striving for international understanding.

Many people tried hard to make a success of ILSCAE. Its objectives remain a challenge to future generations of adult educators. The new world of information and communications technologies offer possibilities to people in both south and north that were not available to ILSCAE members during the period 1984–94. Indeed, the writing of this chapter, which has called on the memories and views of a considerable number of people across the world, could not have happened without these new possibilities.

Appendix 1 Inviting views about ILSCAE

You may find these headings helpful in order to organise your thoughts:

- What were the unique features of ILSCAE?
- What were the strong points of ILSCAE?
- What were its weaknesses?
- What was the personal significance of involvement in ILSCAE for you?
- Looking back over the purposes of ILSCAE, which do you think are the most important?
- Are there some aims which you do not personally agree with?

- Are there other international bodies which now cover the same ground as ILSCAE did in the past?
- Is there anything else you want to say about ILSCAE?

Appendix 2 The conferences

Year	Country and place	Host organisation
1984	USA, New Jersey	Rutgers University
1985	Sweden, Stockholm/Gothenburg	Sanga-Saby and Ljungskile folk high schools
1986	England, Nottingham	University of Nottingham
1987	Netherlands, Bergen	Bergen folk high school
1988	Canada, Toronto	Ontario Institute for Studies in Education
1989	Nicaragua, Managua	Popular Education Department of the Ministry of Education
1992	Northern Ireland, Derry	Magee College, University of Ulster
1993	Tunisia, Tunis	Education Department of the Palestine Liberation Organisation
1994	Slovenia, Lake Bled	Slovene Adult Education Centre

References

Barr, J. (1999) *Liberating Knowledge: Research, Feminism and Adult Education*, NIACE

Castells, M. (1998) *End of Millennium*, Blackwells

Collins, M. (1991) *Adult Education as Vocation: A Critical Role for the Adult Educator*, Routledge

Foley, G. (1995) *Understanding Education and Training*, Allen and Unwin

ILSCAE (1987) *About a Week in Nottingham: Themes from the 1986 Conference of the International League for Social Commitment in Adult Education*, Clapham-Battersea Adult Education Institute

ILSCAE (1989) *Finding Our Voices...Seeing With New Eyes: Themes from the 1988 ILSCAE Conference, Toronto, Canada*, Institute of Technical and Adult Teacher Education

ILSCAE (1996) *Adult Learning and Power: The 8th Annual ILSCAE Conference, Bled, Slovenia, June 26 to July 3, 1994*, Slovene Adult Education Centre

Newman, M. (1994) *Defining the Enemy: Adult Education in Social Action*, Stewart Victor Publishing

Welton, M. (ed) (1995) *In Defence of the Lifeworld: Critical Perspectives on Adult Learning*, State University of New York Press

Section II
Promoting curriculum change

8   Beyond the borders of study skills and personal development

Kenneth Gibson

Introduction

From September 1995 to September 1999 the Centre for Access and Lifelong Learning at the University of Derby provided co-ordination for two projects funded under GRUNDTVIG, the European Commission's SOCRATES Adult Education Initiative. The first project, Access to European Studies for Adult Learners (ASEAL), which was completed in August 1997, saw the development of four European Studies modules, in English, French, German and Spanish, and one module written in English for Greek students. The aim of the second project, Capabilities for Progression in Adult Education (CAPAE), which started in September 1997, was to develop study skills and personal development modules at a range of levels and in a number of languages with each institution developing them to their own context and requirements (Reed, 1997).

The type of work carried out on the CAPAE project has been described elsewhere, but a brief explanation of the main elements of the programme is necessary to illustrate the diversity of approaches employed by the participating institutions (Gibson 1998). Four educational institutes took part in the project: the University of Derby; the Zentrum für Weiterbildung (Centre for Continuing Education) in Frankfurt am Main, Germany; University of Deusto in Bilbao, Spain; Omega-Tsakalou Institute in Thessalonika, Greece and the Chamber of Commerce in Rodez, France. The partner in Germany developed modules to meet the needs of young female migrants, or children of migrants, who needed to develop skills to gain access to vocational courses. In France, the target group were unemployed 18–26 year-olds, who needed to enhance their job search techniques. The Spanish partner forged links with the Basque Regional Government and the Association of Parents of Children of Vizcaya, to attract other learners alongside their established group of pensioners who were the focus of the project. The partner in Greece chose to develop modules in English because of their link with an English university and because a large component of their students worked in the catering industry serving tourists from all over the world. The University of Derby developed modules to be integrated into their Access course for a wide range of learners returning to education.

It is generally recognised that working together on a transnational project can be problematic, and numerous barriers and problems have to be overcome throughout its life. For example, Paolo Federighi identifies a 'notable skills gap in the transnational dimension of adult education', and he also points to a lack of knowledge in 'the ability to understand the plurality of educational and cultural models operating in northern and southern Europe', or, as he puts it more simply, 'cultural barriers' (EAEA 1997, 30). John Field has also identified barriers such as language, time, cost and the lack of prior contact with partners (Field 1997, 23). This chapter addresses how some of these problems were overcome in the CAPAE project by drawing on the experiences of the project leader, who was expected to visit the partners at regular intervals throughout the first year.

One of the main advantages of the CAPAE project was the continuity of partnership arrangements. The partners who had previously been involved in the ASEAL project continued to remain partners for the second project. English was already the established form of communication, although many of the colleagues had at least a second, if not a third language. Two years of previous contact allowed a smoother flow of communication in the initial stages, and the preliminaries of 'getting to know each other' were therefore not necessary. There was also a general consensus that study skills and personal development were important educational components that needed to be integrated into the curriculum of each institution.

Some of the more general problems were therefore solved at the beginning but, as the work progressed, more specific problems needed to be addressed. To a certain extent, some of them were anticipated from the outset, but effective ways to solve them became an integral part of the learning process for everyone. Before going on to discuss these problems, a brief description of the social background of the students and the educational priorities of each institution is given, which illustrates how all the partners had a different mission, a different set of circumstances and a particular pedagogical approach.

The students and the institutions

The social backgrounds of the students in each institution were extremely diverse. At one end of the spectrum we find a small businessman in Greece, wishing to update his skills for business purposes, and at the other end a young woman from Iran just granted political asylum who wanted to develop skills to find work. As mentioned above, the partner in Spain had attracted retired workers from the Basque region who wished to expand on existing skills and develop new ones. The partner in France was working together with a specific age group of unemployed youngsters, mainly drawn from middle-class backgrounds. The cohort in Derby came from a very wide range of social backgrounds, with ages ranging from 21–70.

The educational context was as varied as the social and priorities differed to the extreme. For example, the partner in Spain wished to write the modules in the context of leisure studies, which was eventually achieved with great success. The Greek partner had to consider the needs of people from marketing and journalism, who were studying alongside older people from the catering and service industries. The German partner had to tackle the difficulties of teaching individuals from different countries who all spoke different languages and were at various levels in their educational development. The partnership, therefore, centred around diverse developments of a particular idea that would be adopted appropriately for the context and targets groups of each partner.

Clarifying terms and concepts

The first problem that had to be tackled was to clarify and define the terms 'study skills and personal development' and to establish a mutual understanding of their usage. It was also imperative to discuss how the modules were to be developed within each partner's political, educational and social context. Although the Omega-Tsakalou Institute did deliver an adapted key skills module for the benefit of those students who wished to embark on a course in England, most of the partners, with the exception of the University of Derby and the Greek partner, had little experience in delivering skills and development units. In the partner institutions it was also rare to find the support mechanisms normally available to adult students, such as child-care facilities, learning support and on-course guidance.

The initial discussions with colleagues, therefore, focussed on a sharing of perceptions, and an exchange of views and ideas on the concept of adult education. Out of these discussions it became clear that each partner would have to develop the modules according to the needs of their own particular learners and to design them to fit into their own teaching curricular. It is also worth mentioning that these discussions dispelled the fear expressed by some of the partners that the co-ordinating institute wished to impose its own views and ideas on how the partners should develop the modules.

In the lecture halls

For the next step it was decided that the project leader, who was employed by the co-ordinating institution on a part-time basis to network between partners, should go into the lecture halls and deliver either a study skills or personal development session. This was done to investigate students' perceptions and understanding of these terms. What made this approach most fruitful and enjoyable was the discovery, for example, that a self-employed chef running a small taverna on the Greek coastline understood personal development to be a means whereby he could find ways to encourage his staff to offer a more satis-factory service to foreign nationals. In contrast to this, it was agreed with some retired industrial workers from Bilbao that personal development at the age of 65 was not impossible, but a way to make their retirement just as productive as their working life. Moreover, with a group of unemployed youngsters in France it took very little persuading that to develop one's writing and presenta-tion skills would greatly enhance their prospects for progression to study or employment. In contrast to this, the main priority of the young women immi-grants in Germany was to find out how their peers perceived them when working together on group projects.

The results of the classroom sessions were then discussed with colleagues and it was decided to conduct a needs analysis, by the use of questionnaires, and after this to involve the learners themselves in the development of the modules. Thus, the learners discussed their skills and development needs in small groups and the results were analysed and brought to larger discussion groups. These activities were found to be fruitful for both students and tutors, and the feedback was extremely positive. The students expressed their satisfac-tion with the whole process and described how the discussions had given them the feeling of shared responsibility for the needs of each other. From a peda-gogical viewpoint the tutors were pleased with the interaction between them and the students, and it was found that their involvement in the decision-making process stimulated an autonomous approach to learning and played a decisive role in confidence building.

The problem of communication

The second problem that had to be overcome was the maintenance of an effec-tive communication system between partners. This was not so much a language problem, but more a problem of stimulating continued interest in the project and keeping in touch over great distances and long periods of time. There was certainly a willingness to build some form of close network and it was apparent, on a personal level, that the individuals who had decided to work on the project were committed to completing the work. There were, however, a number of constraints placed on the partners by the amount of responsibili-ties they had on a day-to-day level in their own organisations. All the colleagues from Greece, Germany, France and Spain had administrative and teaching commitments to fulfil and the European project tended to be placed on the back burner until a later date.

For the co-ordinating institute, this proved very frustrating and it became difficult at certain times to keep the project moving. Despite the effective use of all the means of technological communication – email, internet, fax and telephone – it proved very difficult to retain the interest that all partners had demonstrated on the initial visits. It was only through the sub-group meetings or symposia, which were held at regular intervals and at different locations, that the initial interest could be rekindled and the partners motivated to complete the work. The symposia were also important because of the social activities and the forging of links, not only with colleagues working on the project, but also with other academic and support staff who were interested or involved in the European dimension of adult education.

This contact proved to be one of the most satisfying aspects of the project as ideas could be discussed on a much broader level above and beyond the confines of the SOCRATES programme. Thus, although communication remained difficult throughout the project, one's own personal and professional development was greatly enhanced by meeting with colleagues working in different professional and educational contexts.

The question of partnership

In the literature of the SOCRATES programme published by the European Commission there is scant mention of the whole question of partnership and how this should function. In the guidelines for applicants it was stated that all partners should actively contribute 'by pooling their expertise in the conception, implementation and evaluation of the project; as well as ensuring the dissemination of the results'. Moreover, it is emphasised that the development of each project should 'seek to promote the exchange of experience, information, innovation and good practice … by stimulating active co-operation between the many different partners'. From the experience of working closely with others on this project it can be stated that the above priorities were all achieved, but the question remains open as to whether such projects really stimulate a lasting or long-term European co-operation.

A short-term project like this may forge links and stimulate active co-operation, but in retrospect the partnerships formed are, in reality, only on a very superficial level. This is not the fault of the institutions, or of the individuals involved, but more of the organising body. John Field has already indicated that the European Union (EU) sees lifelong learning 'as a means of achieving two important policy goals'. The first is the overcoming of the consequences of social exclusion and the second is to ensure a 'flexible, adaptable and productive workforce' (Field 1998, 162). This policy suggests that the decision-makers have economic priorities, rather than a policy designed to enhance the quality of life for those groups whom the partners are targeting. It could be argued that the question of partnership should revolve around deepening the links made between partners, and more finances made available for all participants to visit the institutions. This means that the students should also be given the opportunity to travel and meet their counterparts in other countries. This would promote closer links between partners and greatly enhance the European dimension for all involved.

A more intense working relationship between all concerned, made possible by better finance and an extended time to develop the work, would also make it possible, as Federighi argues, 'to give present day adult education a catalytic role building for a new juridical and political order' (EAEA 1997). Of course, the policy makers in the EU are by no means ready to finance such large integrated projects, but the outcomes of such work would be of the greatest benefit to all, not only politically but also socially. More recently, Burns and Schuller have suggested that the quality of relationships between groups can be used to measure social capital, which leads to a better under-standing of the 'relationships between the different forms of learning which contribute to a genuine learning society' (Coffield 1999, 57).

Internal change

The question of internal and institutional change needs to be briefly addressed as these are inevitably effected in all transnational projects. Overall, it was observed that the changes wrought by working with other European partners were minimal. The most significant change was perhaps coping with an extra workload on top of other teaching and administrative duties. This problem could, however, have been overcome by the availability of extra funds to finance additional administrative staff at the partner institutions, not only at the co-ordinating institute.

The question of continued employment was also an issue for most of the partners. At least three colleagues were employed only on part-time fixed term contracts and when either funding was cut or the project ended these individuals were left with the problem of finding employment. This was an unfortunate conclusion to the project, because the experience gained and the contacts made could have been gainfully exploited for future work.

Conclusion

Despite the ups and downs of working together on a European SOCRATES project, the benefits can also be immense. The experience can generate an enormous amount of professional development among those individuals who are involved, and can initiate a process of change and innovation more broadly in the partner organisations. However, for these gains to be lasting ones, there needs to be attention to their sustainability over the longer term. The European Commission, and above all those responsible for the SOCRATES programme do, in particular, need to address the question of continuity. More money needs to be made available for existing partners, to allow institutions to reap the benefits of working together and maintain contact on a longer-term basis.

References

Coffield, F. (ed) (1999) *Why's the Beer Always Stronger Up North? Studies of Lifelong Learning in Europe*, The Policy Press

European Association for the Education of Adults [EAEA] (1997) *The Preparation and Management of Transnational Adult Education Projects*, Amersfoort

European Commission (1997) *Socrates Guidelines for Applicants*, EC

Field, J. (1997) 'Continuing Education and the European Dimension: A Survey of British Professionals' Attitudes', *Journal of Further and Higher Education*, 21, 19–32

Field, J. (1998) *European Dimensions: Education, Training and the European Union*, Jessica Kingsley

Gibson, K. (1998) 'Personalised Pathways for Progression', *Adults Learning*, 10(2), 9–10

Reed, E. (1997) 'Capabilities for Progression in Adult Education Project', *Access Networking*, 6, 14

9 Adult learners' environmental training and resources project: a European partnership

Julie Shaw

Introduction

ALERT – the adult learners' environmental training and resources project – was created to develop environmental education with adult learners in disadvantaged communities. It involved partners from Italy, Austria and Spain; it aimed to promote more active forms of environmental learning, while providing learner support using new technologies, as well as more conventional resources; and it included among its goals the development of the partner institutions as learning organisations. This was an ambitious undertaking, initiated at a time of upheaval in the local authority adult education service. It also required great persistence after what could have been a decisive early rejection. Nevertheless, it appears to have paid huge dividends in terms of active partnership and innovative curriculum development.

The Adult and Community Education Service of Bath and North East Somerset Council succeeded in securing funding from the SOCRATES Adult Education Action of the European Commission, in September 1999, in order to develop an innovative European environmental education project. SOCRATES granted 88,546 Euros for the first year of the project, which enabled the Service to employ a co-ordinator for 12 hours per week, work with partners in developing a European partnership and engage with potential adult learners in the cities and regions of the partner countries.

The partners in the ALERT project are based in Bath (envolve, formerly Bath Environment Centre), Vienna *('die Umweltberatung'/*Environmental Guidance), Venice (*Forum per la Laguna*/Forum for the Lagoon) and Granada (*Centro Internacional de Estudio Urbanos*/International Centre for Urban Studies). All of the partners are Urban Forums for Sustainable Development and were located via the Service's informal partnership with envolve/Bath Environment Centre. The urban forum status is supported by two Directorates-General of the European Commission: the DG for Information, Communication and Culture, and the DG for Environment.

Partners work in a variety of contexts, including education, research and environmental forums. The project aimed:

- To develop the capacity of the partners to work together at the European level;
- To pioneer new and innovative working practices within their organisations;
- To create a European Environmental Education curriculum, piloted with adult learners in each partner region and country in the second year of the project.

The ALERT Project: aiming for innovation in adult education

Before outlining the lengthy and somewhat complex issues involved in working at the European level, it is necessary to give a clear summary of the key aims and objectives of the ALERT project. ALERT aims to develop and promote a unique approach to environmental education with adult learners in disadvantaged communities. The common environmental, social and economic themes identified by project partners have formed the context for the project, with the overall aim of creating a European environmental education curriculum, to be piloted with adult learners in each partner region.

Partners have been using a range of multi-media resources in both working together and developing the curriculum. These include on-line conferencing, a partnership Intranet and a SOCRATES ALERT learners' website. Each partner agreed to develop a range of activities to pilot with adult learners. These include courses and programmes of learning based on activities to engage adults with their environment. A modular curriculum has enabled learners to undertake core skills units in ICT (the basics, the internet and web essentials) and study skills (writing, researching, working with information) and introduce them to the languages of the partnership (English, Italian, Spanish and German). Optional units covering a range of environmental concerns (including eco-tourism, discovering your environment, the alternative transport city, sowing and growing) were designed to be appropriate to the culture and working practices of each partner organisation and programme participants. Adult learners were encouraged to communicate with each other via email, conferencing and the SOCRATES ALERT website.

The SOCRATES Adult Education Action

In drafting the proposal, the partners paid close attention to the European Commission's own priorities and thinking (CEC 1997). Unlike the target-driven and output-led impetus of the Structural Funds, such as the European Social Fund, SOCRATES is, generally speaking, more concerned with innovation, partnership, promoting the European dimension and development. The European Commission White Paper on Education and Training (CEC 1995) stressed the need for the 'European dimension' to be integral to education in raising awareness and strengthening cohesion within the member states, and also alluded to the wealth of traditions that need to be preserved.

After 1995, the Commission's training and education programmes, LEONARDO and SOCRATES, were both reviewed in the light of the aims and objectives put forward by the White Paper. The Adult Education Action, launched under the SOCRATES programme in 1995, was designed to allocate grants to two types of project, focusing on either the promotion and knowledge of Europe, or the enhancement of education through European co-operation. From the outset of the programme, the SOCRATES Guidelines allowed for a great variety of potential project content and outcomes, with emphasis placed on the promotion of quality adult education though exchanges of experience, innovation and good practice at a European level.

Whilst there is considerable scope within this remit, working procedures and eligible institutions, the Adult Education Action requires that each project has a transnational partnership between organisations from at least three member states, and makes it clear that every partner must participate actively in the project. Besides the European character, which must be emphasised in every case, the success of an application depends on a number of additional criteria, according to which priority is given to projects considered to be innovative and lend themselves to the sharing of experience. There is an emphasis on aiming to develop specific products – ie training modules, guides, etc and for dissemination to have a potential 'high multiplier' effect. Projects must include high-quality evaluation arrangements, and involve a range of organisations and a broad constituency of target groups.

First steps

Initially, the ALERT partnership was successful in securing a grant from the SOCRATES Adult Education Action solely for a preparatory visit. Preparatory visits are intended to allow potential partners, with a potentially promising idea, to work up a full, detailed proposal. The initial grant covered the travel expenses, accommodation and basic subsidence costs involved in physically meeting in Bath, where the Adult and Community Education Service hosted a series of meetings and development workshops in order to try and develop project ideas with partners.

Discussion and sharing of the various partner organisations' knowledge and experience led to the general conclusion that adults have tended to learn about environmental issues in a didactic manner; and that a structured, integrated approach to environmental education has not been available at a community level. It was this commonly agreed pedagogic and curricular context that underpinned the subsequent development of the project bid.

Learning to understand SOCRATES

The ALERT project application did not fully satisfy the qualitative criteria required by SOCRATES when it was first submitted in 1997. This decision was not a straightforward rejection of the project bid as such, and in retrospect it seems to have been an outcome of not being familiar with the ethos of the SOCRATES programme at the time when the application was written. Our previous experience at the European level for the Adult and Community Education Service was focused on the European Social Fund, and the European dimension and developmental processes of SOCRATES were not fully understood at this stage.

This understanding did not come immediately. The Service needed to use some initiative and sought feedback, initially from the National Agency for SOCRATES in London, and then from the SOCRATES Technical Assistance Office in Brussels. An input of pump-priming money from Bath and North East Somerset Council was then needed in order for the Service to prepare the necessary background work to take to a one-to-one in-depth consultation at the SOCRATES Office in Brussels. During this meeting, a number of suggestions were made on how the bid could be improved in order for it to be resubmitted for consideration in 1999. The most beneficial outcome of the consultation came in understanding the philosophy behind the SOCRATES action, resulting in a bid much more closely aligned with the programme's ethos and purposes. We also learned that persistence, and a willingness to make personal contact, were worth the effort.

Partnership

In the first year, the ALERT project focused on the development of the partnership and the capacity of partners to develop as learning organisations. Communication within the partnership has been both virtual and actual, including extensive use of email, online conferencing and a 'physical' meeting for a development workshop in Vienna. At this stage it was becoming evident that language barriers, different cultures, working practices and expectations were the most potentially difficult areas to navigate in co-ordinating an international project. Expectations from the co-ordinating partner, and indeed from the SOCRATES programme itself, are very much weighted to the precise delivery of the project, particularly in respect of financial returns and reporting mechanisms. Whilst this is an essential ingredient in the fair and accountable delivery of the project, it can be an onerous task to agree on the ways in which each partner fulfils this side of the partnership agreement.

There is also a danger that each partner has a very clear and firm idea of how the project is going to be delivered by themselves and their organisation.

In a project that is very much about the development of a partnership at the European level, enabling potential adult learners to feed into the development process and the piloting of these ideas to assess their viability, it can be counter-productive to have a pre-set agenda for the project. Each partner has a different perspective on how these objectives are to be achieved and, in some instances, may not be prepared or able to allow for the flexibility required. A willingness to compromise is essential.

On a more positive note, an actual physical meeting is so much more effective in tackling these potentially thorny issues. At the development work-shop in Vienna, it became clear that each partner needs to have the understanding, space and capacity to develop the project in their own contexts, whilst not losing sight of the key aim of working at the European level. This does place a heavy burden on the project co-ordinating organisation, which must steer very carefully and sensitively to ensure that this happens, whilst fulfilling the project's aims and objectives and satisfying the criteria set out in the SOCRATES programme. In the midst of all this, the needs of the educa-tion context, the subject and the potential learners can sometimes be overwhelmed by the politics of managing the assertion of each organisation in turn!

Developing a European partnership for environmental adult education

This was an ambitious undertaking: being involved in transnational projects at all is demanding and challenging on a number of levels (Blackley, Seymour and Goddard 1997). First, there are constraints in terms of resources, which are tested when innovative and transnational projects stretch the limits of staffing and financial assets. Second, it is a test of the capacity for staff and organisations to cope with new types of ideas and working practices, and in understanding other people, organisations and cultures.

However, the benefits to be gained from working transnationally are many: it can present the opportunity to develop a project idea within a poten-tially new sphere and framework; it may build the capacity of the organisations' staff and systems; it can provide strategic benefit to the organisations, their staff, their target groups and the wider sector. In particular, international experience can enrich the organisation through working in partnership with organisations in other countries, in terms of support, joint working, further projects and access to new ideas, techniques and networks.

References

Blackley, S., Seymour, H. and Goddard, M. (1997) *Innovative and Transnational Projects: A Guide for Organisations Running Projects Supported by the European Structural Funds, Community Action*

Programmes, or Other European Commission Sources, Industrial Common Ownership Movement

CEC (1995) *Teaching and Learning: Towards the Learning Society*, Office for Official Publications of the European Union, Commission of the European Communities

Commission of the European Communities (1997) *The European Union and the Environment*, Office for Official Publications of the European Union

10 Building a European dimension in trade union education

Jeff Bridgford

The European challenge to trade union education

The 'Europeanisation' of industrial relations is gathering pace. Capital has become increasingly mobile, and the development of European (and indeed global) companies has had a significant impact on national patterns of industrial relations. Moreover, the European Union (EU) has itself become a significant actor in the field of industrial relations in Europe. It is important as a legislator, whose Directives have formed the basis for law in the member states on such issues as health and safety, equal opportunities, atypical work and European Works Councils. It is also a powerful policy-maker, notably with the emergence of the Single European Market, the introduction of the Euro and the European Employment Strategy, and as a facilitator of a 'Social Dialogue', involving a process of discussions and negotiations between European trade unions and employers' organisations. As a result of these shifts, as well as the general Europeanisation of the economy, a European industrial relations system is beginning to emerge.

This process of Europeanisation has thrown up a series of challenges for trade union organisations. The European Trade Union Confederation (ETUC) has responded in a number of ways:

- By improving its own representativity, which means that it now speaks as an authoritative and credible interlocutor in discussions and negotiations at the European level on behalf of 57 million working people drawn from 85 affiliated organisations (seven national trade union confederations, six observers and 14 European Industry Federations), and coming from 28 countries;
- By negotiating with the employers' organisations, UNICE and CEEP, a series of European framework agreements on such issues as parental leave, part-time work and fixed-term contracts;
- By developing a series of strategies and policies addressing a wide range of European industrial relations issues, notably the development of a co-ordinated European collective bargaining policy and the strengthening of the information and consultation procedures of European Works Councils.

Europeanisation has led to significant changes in the demands placed upon trade union officers and representatives, producing new training needs within trade union organisations. As a result, the ETUC has agreed a strategic training policy that aims to develop a European trade union identity and to provide training for the leading actors of the European trade union movement.

It has also set up two training agencies to carry out this work. The Association for European Training of Workers on the Impact of New Technology, normally known by its French acronym AFETT, was established in 1986 to provide specialised training in the analysis of the social and organisational implications of new technologies, as a means of assisting trade union negotiations in the context of technological change. The European Trade Union College (ETUCO) was established in 1990 and was given a broader remit: to devise training programmes for the ETUC as a whole, and to ensure that proper account was taken of the European dimension in trade union education at all levels. Whilst remaining separate organisations they have now developed a high level of synergy and co-operation, thus ensuring a coherent approach to European trade union education.

The work of the ETUCO

The core of ETUCO/AFETT work is the provision of short courses for European trade union officers and representatives. Over the years ETUCO/AFETT has delivered and co-ordinated hundreds of European courses reflecting key ETUC policy priorities, addressing such topics as: economic and monetary union; social dialogue; equal opportunities; collective bargaining at the European level; working time; atypical work; the future of public services in Europe; social protection; health and safety at work; cleaner technology; and information society. In addition, ETUCO/AFETT has provided a vast range of tailor-made courses in response to the changing needs of ETUC affiliates – courses on a wide range of sectoral issues, particularly relating to the social consequences of industrial and technological change; courses to enable new EU members and new ETUC members (notably those from the countries of central and eastern Europe) to integrate more readily into European trade union activities; language learning courses to improve communications between European trade unionists (English, French and German); courses to enhance strategic and project management skills; and courses in response to emerging policy priorities, above all, the creation of European Works Councils.

In addition, ETUCO/AFETT offers a 'long' course, the European Training Course, for young trade union officers soon to be faced with the challenge of European trade union activities. This course, three residential weeks held over a 12 month period, aims to provide an understanding of the latest developments affecting European trade unionism and an opportunity for improving certain operational skills. The first week provides a comparative background. Participants present national experiences of workplace representation and collective bargaining, and become more aware of what is happening beyond their own national borders. The second week, held in Brussels, provides an opportunity to visit the institutions of the EU, the ETUC, the European Industry Federations and also the employers' organisation UNICE. This helps in ensuring a better understanding of the ways in which EU decisions are taken, and of the ways in which trade unions can expect to influence this decision-making process. This second week also provides an opportunity to examine in detail a number of themes, notably employment and unemployment, and to work on European trade union responses. In order to improve understanding of this process, a number of training exercises enable participants to prepare their visits and their discussions with the representatives of the different institutions. In the third week participants are presented with some of the elements of EU social policy and are encouraged to work on European trade union responses to these different policies. In addition, participants are encouraged to examine the relationship between Europe and the rest of the world.

In this way, thousands of trade union officers and representatives from all over Europe have been able to take advantage of a European learning experience. They have been able to acquire new elements of information, notably by comparing aspects of different national industrial relation systems and by becoming acquainted with latest developments at the European level, or latest policy positions of European trade union organisations. In some of the courses, or in some parts of these courses, they have been able to develop new skills: the preparation of action plans for future trade union work at the national and/or European levels; the use of electronic communications; and the learning of foreign languages. In addition, they have been offered a rare opportunity to share European trade union values and to gain a broader European perspective on trade union issues.

With ETUCO/AFETT offices in Brussels and course participants coming from different countries throughout Europe, one particular challenge is to ensure all needs are met. Consultation needs to be extensive, and the planing process needs to be inclusive. At the outset, the ETUC secretariat, in consultation with the Director of ETUCO/AFETT, decides the political priorities, which are then turned into a training programme. ETUCO/AFETT then sends out the training programme to ETUC-affiliated organisations, inviting them to form partnerships to deliver the various courses. The next stage requires partner organisations to propose trainers who are not only able to work in a transnational training environment, but also able to articulate the needs of future course participants. Under the guidance of ETUCO/AFETT, these trainers then meet to redefine the course content and most appropriate methods – who does what and how. Where appropriate and where possible, good practice would also suggest that once they have been enrolled, course participants should be contacted in advance to see how best they can benefit from a particular course.

Developing a curriculum

In order to reinforce the quality of these European training activities and to strengthen the European dimension of national trade union education, ETUCO/AFETT has been involved in three interconnected initiatives: networking of training departments and trainers; production and dissemination of training resources, and provision of an EU information service for education and training projects.

Through a process of networking training departments from affiliated organisations, ETUCO/AFETT has established a unique European trade union education community – a forum for the strategic development of European trade union education and for the articulation of the different levels of European trade union education. This forum provides a channel for the transfer of ETUC political priorities into training activities, and an opportunity for advising on ETUC affiliated organisations' own training needs. In this way it has been possible to establish a common cultural framework ensuring minimum standards for training activities and to engage in a Europe-wide confidence building exercise that has proved to be an essential prerequisite for other joint activities, such as the design and delivery of other European trade union education projects.

Within this European trade union education community ETUCO/ AFETT has developed teaching and learning methodologies that take into account the different cultural backgrounds of European trade unionists and are, therefore, suitable for different transnational training environments. These have been constantly reviewed in the light of further experience and have been distilled into training manuals, the latest of which addresses the challenges for trainers inherent in open and distance learning. European trade union education courses have traditionally been residential, and the face-to-face training methodologies have been beneficial for mutual understanding and the creation of collective European trade union values. More recently, ETUCO/AFETT has started to examine ways in which course delivery could be supported by new distance learning techniques, and has prepared a number of projects to support training for trainers, European Works Council representatives and language learners. It remains to be seen what benefits these new distance learning techniques will bring to European trade union education.

ETUCO/AFETT has also offered a series of pedagogical courses (training Euro-trainers, needs analysis) and workshops (materials development, language learning, evaluation). These events have been designed to reinforce the ETUCO/AFETT network of Eurotrainers by developing shared notions of best pedagogical practice, and by offering regular training opportunities for trainers to update their own knowledge and skills. In more specific terms, a recent training Euro-trainers course aimed to reinforce European co-operation in the framework of trade union training, by developing a methodology adapted to European programmes with particular reference to the debate on distance learning in a trade union environment; a language learning workshop aimed to establish shared networks of best practice in the integration of language training and trade union education activities, and to discuss the use of multimedia in language learning for trade unionist; and a materials workshop aimed to consider the implications of electronic publishing on the develop-ment and dissemination of training materials for European trade union education, and to consider the types of materials to be jointly developed for use at the national level. In addition, and in response to special needs, ETUCO/AFETT has set up projects to develop trade union education networks in the countries of central and eastern Europe (CEEC) – networks that are designed to analyse and exchange experience of trade union education programmes, promote trade union education at all levels, and reinforce CEEC trade unions' educational capacities.

ETUCO/AFETT has also developed its work on training resources and produced its own materials. One example is *Europe and the World of Work*, a set of briefings covering European issues (institutions of the EU, workers organisa-tions, employees' organisations, social dialogue, decision-making at the community level, social policy, economic and monetary union, working time, equal opportunities), which are accompanied by a series of training units. Another example is *Resources for European Works Councils*, which includes materials on the Directive, a simulation exercise, transparencies to explain different systems of worker representation, materials to gain a better under-standing of basic financial information, materials to influence company decisions concerning relocations, closures, outsourcing and investment (for further details about ETUCO/AFETT training resource see www.etuc.org/etuco/en/resources).

These training resources have been designed for use at the European and national levels. The challenge is to ensure that they meet the needs of trainers and learners who are working in different contexts, and who are affected by widely varying cultures, and levels of experience, as well as by different indus-trial relations systems. Good practice would suggest that the process of production is significant for the quality of the materials and for their subse-quent dissemination. One example will suffice. A project to publish a resource book *Trade union education and the environment* was done in two stages. The first stage required the distribution of a questionnaire to tutors and educators working with European trade unions, seeking details of their work in the field of environmental education. Responses to the questionnaire provided the basis for a draft document outlining good practice in this area of work across Europe. The second stage involved holding a European workshop, which was attended by tutors and experts from nine countries and representing thirteen organisations. The draft document was discussed in workshops and plenary sessions, and teaching activities were piloted in transnational groups. The draft version of the resource book was subsequently amended to take into account the experience gained during the workshop. The resource book was intended to serve as a practical tool to support the work of trainers at the national level, and as a synthesis of good practice in the field of environmental education in various countries. It also contained suggestions as to how environmental education could be integrated into other trade union education activities, together with a series of suggested teaching activities, which were designed to be adapted for use at the national level. A model course on *The Workplace and the Environment* was also included.

It has, however, become increasingly clear that paper-based materials have a limited usefulness, and ETUCO/AFETT has changed its publication policy and started to move towards electronic publishing. As a result, training resources can be disseminated more quickly and easily, and trainers can use them in more flexible ways.

In addition to the publication of training resources, ETUCO/AFETT plays an important role in the dissemination of information about existing materials. As a result, the European Trade Union Education Resource Centre (ETUERC) was set up. At a materials workshop, which was attended by trade union education specialists from a number of ETUC affiliated organisations, the criteria for the selection of materials to be included in the database were established. At a further materials workshop, the pilot database was partially redesigned to make it more useful for trainers looking for a particular type of material for a particular target group. As a result, searches on the ACCESS database can be conducted in a wide range of fields, including keywords, language, format, title, author, or combinations of these. The database includes references to published materials, as well as unpublished ETUCO and AFETT course materials, and so constitutes a burgeoning archive of materials for European trade union education. At first, trainers from affiliated organisations were able to request that searches be conducted on their behalf from a distance, or during visits to ETUERC in Brussels. From 1999 onwards this database became an online service available on the ETUCO/AFETT website (www.etuc.org/etuco/en/resources/ETUERC).

ETUCO/AFETT has established an EU information service that offers information and advice on a range of EU programmes and funding opportunities, the aim of which is to support European trade union education projects. It provides a number of online facilities; an information library that includes simple introductions to EU programmes and budget lines, as well as official documents, calls for proposals, application forms and agreements to the Europe server; a help desk, which gives answers to frequently asked questions about potential sources of EU funding for trade union education projects and which offers detailed assistance to trainers seeking to write applications and manage EU-funded education and training projects; and a projects forum that provides online discussions for exchanging ideas and advice on European trade union education and training projects.

In this way, ETUCO/AFETT has been able to set up co-operative part-nerships between ETUC-affiliated organisations that contribute to the development of trade union education at the European level. Moreover, ETUCO/AFETT has successfully managed a series of key projects which have, *inter alia*, reinforced the use of computer-based communications, and enhanced the European Union Information Service (ETUE-net); developed training materials and introductory courses for trade union officers in using the Internet (TRAINS); produced foreign language learning materials; set up partnerships between trade union education departments in Eastern Europe with their counterparts in Western Europe; improved project management skills; assisted the process of training on environmental issues; and developed an online system for distance education in European trade unions (ETUDE). Further-more, ETUCO/AFETT has been a partner in a series of projects co-ordinated by ETUC affiliated organisations and in this way has made available its own expertise, notably in the field of transnational training, intercultural communi-cation and Europe-wide dissemination.

Concluding remarks

In response to the Europeanisation of industrial relations, the ETUC has defined a training policy that aims to develop a European trade union identity and to provide training from the leading actors in the European trade union movement. The ETUC has also set up two training agencies, ETUCO and AFETT, to carry out this policy. The main vehicle for achieving these aims has been the provision of hundreds of European courses, which have been devel-oped in partnership with ETUC affiliated organisations and have provided an opportunity for thousands of trade union officers and representatives from all over Europe to come together to take advantage of a European learning expe-rience. In addition, ETUCO/AFETT has been involved in the networking of training departments and trainers, the production and dissemination of training resource and the provision of an EU information service for education and training projects – all the activities have been designed to reinforce the quality of European training activities and strengthen the European dimension of national trade union education.

Section III
Involving new learners

11 Disabled students: learning, training and Europe

David French

To ensure that opportunities which are open to non-disabled people are not denied to anyone purely on the grounds of disability is an important goal of UK public policy. With the increasing significance of Europe as part of the context within which people build their working lives, it is accordingly important that disabled people are not denied opportunities to encounter European dimensions in their education and training. But perceptions of disability that are based upon what disabled people cannot do, rather than what they can, are heavily ingrained in British culture, as they are also in the rest of Europe. And this continually gives rise to barriers to achieving the objectives of inclusive education and training. This chapter explores how such misconceptions can limit the opportunity for disabled students to gain from European dimensions in their programmes, and considers ways of overcoming them.

The chapter begins with a brief examination of the distinctiveness of British approaches to disability, particularly in relation to education and training. The UK has, despite continuing shortcomings, gone considerably further towards inclusiveness than many other European countries. One useful way of conceptualising the different approaches to disability is represented in the distinction between the 'social' and 'medical' models, the former of which sees 'disability' as a social stereotype, a label that is crudely applied to some people, denying them opportunities open to others. Those approaches often defined as 'medical' see disability as a condition produced as a direct consequence of impairment. In practical terms, the social model emphasises autonomy and independence; the medical model dependency and institutional support. The public language in which disability policy is discussed in the UK is now very much that of the social model, even if policy implementation is often not consistent with it. Useful summaries of disability theory are available in, for example, Oliver (1996) and Davis (1997).

The next section reviews European policies. It is substantially based upon experience of a series of transnational projects at Coventry University and considers the potential of European programmes, together with practical advice for project developers. The chapter concludes with a note on European differences in perceptions and representations of disability.

Disability, disabled students and the British educational system

A recent government 'See the Person' campaign used posters, television adver-
tisements and other media to promote positive images of disabled people. What
made the campaign distinctive was its attempt to use stereotyped images of
disabled people in ways designed to subvert the 'normal', stereotyped, response
to disability. Its viability depended upon at least a minimal level of sophistica-
tion amongst its audience in their perception of disability: it could only work if
attitudes were already changing. That the government should have felt confident enough of this assumption to engage in such a high-profile campaign is an
important indicator of the position in the UK.

The experience of disabled students in British education was, for many
years, one of denied opportunities. Until recently, access routes to university
were available only to the determined and exceptional few. In this respect,
higher education (HE) embodies the structural prejudice that characterises
other parts of the educational system; so action to change the position in HE
can be taken as substantially representative of the wider position across the
education and training system (see Hurst, forthcoming and Owen-Hutchison,
1998, for background). In particular, the Higher Education Funding Council
for England (HEFCE) and the other national UK funding agencies have implemented a number of special programmes that are designed to promote access
for disabled people.

By 2001, there had been four rounds of special HEFCE funding to
develop initiatives to improve the access opportunities for disabled students in
terms of admissions, facilities and academic progress. From 2000–01 HEFCE
specifically allocated an additional 'premium' within the student numbers
element of each institution's block grant, in order to provide a direct financial
incentive to improve the recruitment of disabled students. The Disabled
Students Allowance is also crucial in enabling more students to achieve something like their real potential (DfEE 1998).

This process has led to significant organisational changes. Most universities
and larger colleges now have dedicated offices providing support for disabled
students, and academic staff seeking to meet their needs. All now have formal
policy statements in relation to disability and the Quality Assurance Agency's
Code of Conduct with respect to disabled students will be incorporated in its
routine visits to universities and to course teams. Overall recruitment figures
have improved somewhat, with current figures showing 4 per cent of under-
graduate entry as declaring a disability at the point of application (HESA 1999).

Research at Coventry shows that the full integration of disabled students
requires significant re-evaluation by institutions and academic staff of their
routine, taken-for-granted practices (Earle, et al 1999). This conclusion will
apply equally in further education colleges and elsewhere in the lifelong

learning system. Good teaching methods make a big contribution, but cannot be relied upon as the secret of effective learning for all disabled students. What works well for the student with dyslexia may be quite opposed to that best suited to a student who is blind, or hard of hearing.

A recent survey (Earle, *et al* 1999) shows that some adjustments of practice have almost become routine in English universities, for example allowing extra time in exams for dyslexic students and the provision of sheltered examination conditions. But other potential changes ask serious questions of academic staff. For example, do all building students have to make site visits, whether or not they plan to work on one? How far can or should practical lab sessions be adapted for students with visual impairments? To what extent can subjects traditionally assessed through essays be adapted to meet the needs of students for whom writing may be problematic? These questions are not easily resolved; they exemplify the ways in which British academic staff are increasingly required to distinguish the core academic aims of their programmes from the assumed 'normal' modes of delivery.

The issues for disabled students seeking experience in universities and colleges abroad are evident. If the process of change in UK universities is slow and difficult, what will happen in another country, where the disabled student is not one of an increasingly important constituency within the university system, but a lone, foreign, individual presenting unfamiliar and difficult problems?

European policy

Since the early 1980s, the promotion of student mobility within Europe has been a main Commission aim. First ERASMUS and then SOCRATES have stimulated a position in which the opportunity to spend part of one's course studying abroad has become increasingly a normal choice throughout the educational structure. It is available to students widely through European educational systems, connecting British institutions with partners of all kinds and from all over the continent. But to what extent can disabled students, at whatever stage of the lifelong learning process they may be, take advantage of this opportunity?

A first conclusion is that the numbers doing so are almost certainly very small and include extremely few students indeed with 'serious' impairments. Although direct statistics are not available, experiential evidence, gathered both through work at Coventry and in contact with experts in other countries, gives confidence in the accuracy of this depressing judgement. Of course, unacceptably low participation rates are the norm for disabled students in advanced education throughout Europe, even in those countries that have made most efforts in this respect. But the rates for European mobility are even lower. This is in spite of the apparently high priority given by the European Commission to improving the position. For example, statements about disability provision are a required part of the reports that institutions must make to SOCRATES, but little helpful information ever seems to reach disabled students. Supplementary grants to cover the needs of students with severe impairments can be available, and institutions are encouraged to allow for the particular needs of disabled students in the allocation of normal funds for student finance. On the other hand, SOCRATES co-ordinators often seem not to know of these provisions.

European mobility is of course challenging for all students, involving financial costs, academic risks, removal from the familiar, and a variety of other social and cultural challenges. To confront these demands with any degree of confidence requires assured intercultural skills, often associated with previous periods of residence abroad. It is particularly difficult for anyone with family or other domestic responsibilities, or who has the need to earn money to support his or her studies. The problems in the UK are exacerbated by the well-known limitations of foreign language learning in the British educational system (French 1996).

Disabled students are far from immune from these difficulties. Those disabled people who are able to progress through the educational system are generally skilled in overcoming adversity and institutional prejudice, but this does not necessarily extend to the acquisition of language and other cross-cultural skills. Students with impairments related to communication are particularly disadvantaged. Study abroad also poses extra problems of a very practical nature. Among the more obvious of these are:

- Travel, using unfamiliar systems and routes;
- Accommodation, particularly if specialist accommodation is required when many university systems do not normally provide student accommodation to the extent found in the UK;
- Campuses, which may be inaccessible or dangerous for students with mobility or visual impairments;
- The absence of specialist expertise of the kind now commonly available in the Student Service Departments of UK universities and colleges.

These are real obstacles. There are ways individuals can combat them, starting by using the available surveys and reviews of current provision (Van Acker 1996a, 1996b and Hurst 1998). These rapidly become out of date, but they remain a useful first resource.

An important problem is that improvement in conditions tends to come, not from long-term planning, but in response to the needs of particular students. To quote a conversation with a Belgian colleague, 'the university won't, of its own accord, put a wheelchair ramp in our building, but it soon would if confronted by the embarrassment of his (*sic*) colleagues lifting an exchange student over the step every day'. The history of progress in British universities has similarly predominantly been one of improvisation in response to pressure, followed only later by anything more systematic. Part of the success of British disabled students studying abroad may perhaps, in the end, have to be measured by the extent to which they act as the catalysts of change in the universities and colleges they visit.

There are bigger problems, however. First, financial and material: at very early stage in planning study abroad, students and their advisers need to check arrangements for the payment of benefits, including the disabled students allowance, during the period outside the UK, together with the availability of additional support from SOCRATES, or other sources. Then it is essential to check the systems for obtaining abroad services that may be required, whether, for example, personal assistance or adaptive technology.

Second, there is the need to ensure a positive learning environment at the host institution. As the numbers of students involved in exchanges increase and the European Commission has become more anxious to control the costs of ERASMUS/SOCRATES, so the procedures for the accreditation of study abroad have become more routinised, with automatic, pre-deter-mined, equivalences increasingly displacing the individual discretion and flexibility previously available. In the UK, talk of 'student-centred' approaches often conceals a quite different reality, but at least it is an acknowledged aspiration. However, the whole concept is distinctly alien in many European countries with their more traditional academic cultures. Meeting the special academic needs of individual disabled students may be very challenging in such circumstances.

To achieve a successful period of study abroad in these circumstances requires careful planning of financial and organisational aspects. Direct liaison between staff at the home institution and sympathetic, informed, supportive, academic staff at the receiving university is essential, combined with a high degree of self-reliance and constructive assertiveness on the part of the student. A preliminary visit, to identify potential problems and plan ways around them, is highly desirable. The EMPLOYABILITY website (www.nrec.org.uk/employability) provides valuable information, links and guidance.

Some other aspects of the SOCRATES programme may be less problem-atic, in that they concern other forms of European contact, shorter periods abroad, or involve the exchange student less in mainstream academic activity. But it is through exchanges that much crucial European experience becomes available to students, and so the issues for disabled students cannot be ducked. And what is true for students also generally holds for disabled staff members involved in academic exchanges.

Programmes within the European Social Fund

Disability is also a prominent theme of European Commission programmes concerned with employment. Some specifically address disability as a basis for discrimination in the labour market. It has, for example, been the special focus first of HORIZON and now of the EQUAL programmes, both part of the European Social Fund (ESF), and belonging to a family of measures designed to support disadvantaged groups.

EQUAL has training as an important priority; improved skill levels are seen as crucial to enabling disabled people to compete in the job market. The large sums of money available can be a crucial source of development finance for pilot projects in lifelong learning. The best direct information sources for readers wishing to explore EQUAL further are the European Commission's EUROPA website (listed in the *European resources on the web* at the end of this book) and that of the European Disability Forum (www.edf-feph.org). Most colleges and universities also have European funding offices from which useful advice can be obtained.

HORIZON and EQUAL projects require transnational European partnerships, and these should include training and employer organisations as well as special interest groups. Getting the partnership right is often the key to success in obtaining funding. But they do not necessarily provide European experience to their trainees. Their principle is that training will be better if it incorporates the experience of partners; there is often no opportunity for trainees to make direct contact with their peers in other countries. In effect, the funding tends to support a loose network of more or less parallel national projects.

Indeed, the process through which programmes are selected can itself obstruct effective collaboration: ESF rules dictated that, although projects could be set up as *transnational* partnerships, the approval of individual partners in HORIZON was at *national* level. It can be very disruptive if a team-member fails to gain national approval. Surviving team members are left trying to grab the best available substitute from a miscellany of 'orphans', potential partners left similarly isolated in European virtual reality.

But, whether by luck or determination, these programmes can lead to important innovations in developing European experience in lifelong learning

---

1.   From 1998 to 2000, Coventry University was in a HORIZON project with partners in France, Italy and Spain. Its main focus was employability in the tourism, hospitality and leisure industries. None of the partners were members of the group with which Coventry had originally built its bid (that early partnership had been sunk by the failure of one member to get national approval). The new project was put together on the basis of fairly crude judgements about parallels in subject matter and target groups, and there were quite remarkable differences even in the money each had allocated for transnational work. Despite such problems, a unique programme of peer-support, using an email discussion group, was designed. Language difficulties were to be addressed through the use of a paid translator, acting as an intermediary facilitator between disabled people in Britain and France wishing to share their experience of employment and training with their peers in another country. The experiment was short-lived and incomplete, but its outcomes will be readily available to others wishing to go further.

This project also has set up a website for disabled people seeking to work at professional levels in the tourism, leisure and heritage industries. Its experience parallels in many ways the work in the Coventry-led LEONARDO project outlined below.

2.   The Surrey Oaklands NHS Trust has a longer experience of HORIZON, with a well-established partnership, involving institutions in Germany, Ireland, Spain and Italy. Its project, Access Tourism, has provided training and work-experience for disabled people seeking to develop careers in the travel business. HORIZON funding allowed the development of travel agencies, offering direct employment to disabled people, together with a network of specialist facilities throughout Europe. This project demonstrates the potential of ESF funding as seed-money for important, long-term, pan-European initiatives.

Coventry and Surrey Oaklands plan to demonstrate how ESF funding can stimulate European dimensions in lifelong learning through new joint projects. Details will be available through the INTOWORK website

for disabled students. Two examples show what can be achieved. ESF funding can be less competitive than other European initiatives, giving a higher chance of success. This is significant, given the heavy time commitment in preparing good project applications. But, to balance this, the financial contribution required from institutions as match funding may be higher.

Other European programmes related to employment and training

The main vehicle providing support for projects in relation to training and employment is the LEONARDO programme. Disability is an important priority in LEONARDO, alongside other areas of equal opportunities. Unlike the ESF programmes, the presence of an explicit element of European experience for trainees is central. Indeed, an important area of LEONARDO is support for transnational industrial training placements. Other projects may offer indirect contact with peers abroad, or access to training material from other countries.

The problems with LEONARDO are that the competition for funding is intense, and (as with all European projects) reporting and project-management requirements are very demanding. It may, therefore, be difficult for newcomers to gain acceptance. But it is open to all organisations that can claim to deliver training, whether in FE, HE, the private sector or the voluntary sector, and it can stimulate important developments, of which the following is perhaps a useful example.

The project, co-ordinated by Coventry University, had partners in Greece and Sweden; its main activity was to produce a website (EMPLOY-ABILITY, address given above) for use by disabled students, graduates and other seeking to build professional-level careers. The site provides special information about the communications industries, but is useful much more widely. It was designed, and is being maintained, as a lifelong learning resource that users will return to as their careers develop. It is available in three parallel versions, prepared for each country and in its own language. Its four sections are:

- Career development support, with some interactive exercises.
- Resource material and advice for those seeking training, education or employment in other European countries.
- Guidance specific to career-building in the communications industries.
- Advice and guidance about resources in relation to welfare benefits, law and other rights.

The site is available free for disabled people seeking work at professional or managerial levels (particularly in the communication industries), as well as anyone advising disabled students about European experience. It contains a feedback facility, the use of which will support updating and revisions.

Preparation of the site, and ensuring that its contents were appropriate to conditions in each country, was both demanding and revealing. It high-lighted the material and, equally importantly, the cultural differences that disabled students seeking to gain experience of other European countries, have to confront. Additional LEONARDO funding is enabling the site to be developed for users in Bulgaria and Cyprus.

European programmes like LEONARDO and those in the ESF, can be good sources of development finance for projects concerned with disability and life-long learning. A concern with equal opportunities is often among the selection criteria, disability is frequently explicitly identified, and lifelong learning is another common area of emphasis. There are therefore good reasons for considering proposals under these programmes. But preparing solid applications is very demanding.

A good idea is not enough unless it also meets the selection criteria. Where transnational partnerships are required, it is often best if these draw on previously established relationships. It is worth trying to join established partnerships with a good track-record: there are directories and databases of previous projects, and the support offices will help. Managing European projects can be immensely arduous and the costs of this must be included in the financial planning. Many European projects require at least 50 per cent match-funding and it is vital to sort this out before putting the application together.

A note on cultural differences in relation to disability

Promoting European dimensions in lifelong learning for disabled people will often require the ability to recognise and negotiate radical differences in the meaning attached to disability in different European countries. There are guides to benefits, legislation and support systems (see the EMPLOYABILITY and INTOWORK websites), but little is published on the area of cultural difference. This is an important absence, given that the reality of disability is mainly determined by the way non-disabled people respond to impairment, rather than the nature of the impairment itself.

Projects led by Coventry's Centre for Research and Policy in Disability have involved the collection of relevant evidence in six contrasting European countries. Although this work has not been entirely systematic, given that it has been within three quite different projects, the general outcome is quite clear. Attitudes that lead to lower expectations of disabled people's abilities and potential tend to be more common in many European countries than in the UK. Disabled people are more likely to be perceived as being passive recipients of services done for them, than active in controlling their own lives. On the other hand, it is also clear that attitudes vary within countries, that they are changing, and that initiatives such as those described above have an important role to play in promoting such change.

Projects will be more likely to make a significant impact if they have the active participation of disabled people, as trainees or members of project management teams. Furthermore, success in obtaining funding for transnational projects is often dependent on having what in Euro-speak are called 'multi-player networks', that is, groupings that bring together partners from the voluntary sector, as well as businesses and institutions sponsored by local or national government. If organisations of disabled people have full and proper roles in such networks, the chances of getting funding and of achieving successful outcomes will be improved. Perhaps equally important is the possibility that new links in partner countries will be stimulated and important change across the states of Europe will be encouraged.

Acknowledgement

The work that has informed this paper has been carried out in the Centre for Research and Policy in Disability and the author wishes to express particular thanks to Mike Adams, Amanda Crowfoot and Kulwant Dhailiwal for their comments on this text.

References

Davis, L. (ed) (1997) *The Disability Studies Reader*, Routledge

DfEE (1998) *Briding the Gap – A guide to the Disabled Students' Allowances (DSAs) in Higher Education*, Department for Education and Employment

Earle, S., Adams, M. and French, D. (1999) 'A National Survey of Assessment Practices in Higher Education: Special Provisions for Students with Disabilities and Learning Difficulties', *Skill Journal*, 65, 22–24

French, D. (1996) 'ERASMUS, SOCRATES and the Myth of the Universal University', *Scottish Communication Association Journal*, 2, 309–328

HESA (1999) *Annual Report*, Higher Education Statistical Agency

Hurst, A. (ed) (1998) *Higher Education and Disabled Students: International Approaches*, Ashgate Publishing

Hurst, A. (ed) (forthcoming) *The Accessible Millennium: Developing Policy and Provision for Disabled Students in Higher Education*, Ashgate Publishing

Oliver, M. (1996) *Understanding Disability: From Theory to Practice*, Macmillan

Owen-Hutchinson, J. *et al* (1998) *Breaking Down Barriers: Access to Further and Higher Education for Visually-Impaired Students*, Stanley Thornes

Van Acker, M. (1996a) *Studying Abroad 1: Checklist of Needs for Students with Disabilities*, Catholic University of Leuven

Van Acker, M. (1996b) *Studying Abroad 2: European Guide for Students with Disabilities,* Catholic University of Leuven

12   The PIMOS project: an example of the benefits from a transnational project

Philip Taylor, Nigel Lloyd, Christine Tillsley and Shree Mandke

Background

The PIMOS (Preventative Initiative to Maintain Occupational Skills) project was designed to identify the learning needs of older professionals, in order to maintain employability and to explore barriers to maintaining employability. The project was co-ordinated by an offshoot of Dresden Technical University and had partners in Belgium and the UK. This chapter describes the process and findings of the project and provides three case studies of how the partners gained benefit. It also identifies the success factors for the project.

The basis for the project was a recognition that workers aged 45 or over are profoundly disadvantaged amid the rapid changes that characterise the European labour market and that, if they are to compete successfully and continue to contribute to the economy, improving and maintaining their employability is a priority for policy makers and for older people themselves. In increasingly competitive global and domestic markets, organisations are changing both structurally and organisationally. Global procurement, intensified competition and strategies for increasing productivity, such as down-sizing, de-layering and out-sourcing, have effectively changed the shape of work. In the case of older workers the impacts have been particularly dramatic. For example, the restructuring of the economy of Eastern Germany since unification has proved most difficult for older workers.

With the drive for cost efficiencies and reductions in overheads, concerns over human resources costs have often led to the replacement of experience and expertise with cheaper and younger colleagues or recruits. Moreover, the desire for individuals to identify with organisational aims and objectives has also meant that many older workers, who are unable or unwilling to adapt to change, have had to leave their jobs. As a result, it is becoming increasingly difficult for many older people to remain in employment.

There is a long-term trend towards declining employment rates among older workers. Older workers are over-represented among the long-term unemployed and there is evidence of widespread age discrimination in the labour market. One manifestation of age-related barriers is that older workers are under-represented among those participating in training activities, with evidence that the problem is in the unwillingness of employers to provide training, rather than lack of demand amongst older people.

However, against a background of population ageing and concerns about rising pension costs, there is increasing interest among policy makers about improving the employability of older workers. This project aimed to increase understanding of the barriers facing older workers and to put forward policy solutions based on the findings of research carried out in Belgium, Germany and the UK.

PIMOS project and team

PIMOS was financed under the European Commission's LEONARDO programme. The project partnership was led by EIPOS (European Institute for Postgraduate Training at the Dresden Technical University). The project ran from December 1997 to November 1999. It investigated the training, development and support needs of older professionals in order to maintain their employability. This might mean remaining within their present career, by gaining new skills or upgrading existing skills, taking a completely new direction with the same employer, moving from a specialist to a generalist role, or moving into self-employment, or possibly into a completely new occupation. The project also aimed to understand the policy context: identifying attitudes and practices towards older workers, evidence of new initiatives on the part of the social partners and structural barriers to greater participation in the labour market among this group.

The project team consisted of: Germany, Uwe Reese of EIPOS, and representatives of Arbeitsamt Dresden (the State Employment Office); Belgium, Adrien Coucke of VION (a training provider set up by local colleges), and Vera Kellens (self-employed consultant); UK, Nigel Lloyd and Shree Mandke of Cambridge Professional Development (CamProf, a small consultancy) and Philip Taylor and Christine Tillsley of the Open University Business School (OUBS).

Project development

The idea for the project came from EIPOS, who had found that older professionals (aged 40 or over) had the most difficulty adapting to competition in the new labour market of the unified Germany. Arbeitsamt agreed to provide data, but were unable to provide continuing membership of the project team. Other members of the team were assembled with more serendipity than method.

VION was invited to become a partner in PIMOS via a Flemish student on a work placement in EIPOS. CamProf joined the team following a chance meeting between Uwe Reese and Nigel Lloyd at a LEONARDO programme 'animation' meeting in Brussels. The UK team came together after CamProf approached a UK organisation representing employers on the issue of age and employment – Employers' Forum on Age – who put them in touch with Philip Taylor of OUBS, whose primary research interest is in age and employment. Adrien Coucke was retiring and so he brought in Vera Kellens, an independent consultant.

Process

The project consisted of three parallel but independent research projects that went at different speeds, plus group meetings. Different policy contexts and labour market conditions in each partner country led to a decision not to be prescriptive in terms of the approaches taken by each project team. In Germany, the research examined the situation of older workers in all sectors in the Dresden region; in Belgium similarly all sectors in Flanders; in the UK a decision was taken to concentrate the research on the experiences of older individuals in the engineering and construction professions throughout the UK.

Data collection activities comprised: a survey of employers; interviews with representatives from relevant industry bodies, with employers; and interviews and group discussions with professionals aged 40 and over, both employed and unemployed. The project also drew upon analysis of secondary data sources.

Each group meeting lasted 2 days and consisted of: reviews of progress and plans; discussion of finance and administration requirements; plans for exploitation of project findings; ideas for future projects; and social and cultural activities (including meals together, guided tours of training institutions and other local sights, opera or concerts)

There was also sharing of information between the teams outside of the setting of formal meetings. For example, the UK team supplied the Belgian team with a questionnaire used in a previous study.

Key findings

The project findings confirm that older workers appear to be struggling to compete in the labour market. However, we identified some older workers who have been much more successful at adapting to changing circumstances than others. A summary of key findings follows:

- Labour market problems facing mature age professionals are common to each country.
- There is evidence of discrimination against this group in each country in terms of access to employment and continuing professional development.

- On-the-job learning (learning from one's work tasks and hobbies rather than more formal training) is important for middle-aged and older professionals.
- Successful career changes usually happen through small incremental changes, by taking opportunities as they appear and building on experience, not through a major off-the-job retraining break.
- Successful changes of direction are 'managed', typically avoiding redundancy, not always involving a change of employer.
- The same career management skills were shown by those who remained with the same employer as by those who successfully moved into new sectors or professions.
- Older professionals tend to move into specialist niches that are in the boundaries and overlaps between professions, often achieving membership of additional professions.
- There is evidence of movement of older workers from large, structured organisations into self-employment and small- and medium-sized enterprises (SMEs).
- Professional institutions and industry bodies are only just beginning to recognise the career management needs of their older members, and have not yet developed a range of support mechanisms.
- The project identified a wide range of learning needs, in particular, IT-related skills and skills related to becoming self-employed.

These lead to the following important conclusions and recommendations:

- Mature-aged professionals need certain 'life skills' related to: grasping opportunities, proactively managing one's own career, and working in SMEs or in self-employment.
- Employers and professional institutions could play a vital role.
- Government support for the achievement of vocational qualifications needs to reflect the incremental extension of skill sets.
- With multiple careers and life-long learning, it is not only school/college/university leavers who are starting a new career; more support is needed in the form of careers advice and labour market information for older workers.

Case studies

The PIMOS partners agreed that the project had been very successful, in terms of the quality of the research, the development of an on-going international partnership, and the consequent initiatives that were initiated.

United Kingdom

For CamProf this project has introduced a wholly new area of expertise, taking the organisation in a new direction, with the development of new projects and clients in the area of age and employment, and the development of new partnerships in Germany, Belgium and the UK. For OUBS, benefits have included the development of new partnerships and increasing expertise in the construction and engineering professions.

A primary benefit of PIMOS in the UK has been the consequent creation of the MaP>IT (Mature-Age Professionals into IT) projects. These were developed primarily by CamProf, with support from the ITNTO (Information Technology National Training Organisation) who had no programme for the recruitment of older workers. MaP>IT consists of four projects that received £950,000 from the European Social Fund Objective 4 programme. Three of the projects aim to provide IT skills to mature-age professionals with construction and engineering backgrounds, while the fourth consists of a research project examining the barriers facing older engineering and construction professionals entering IT professions and helping career self-management by developing models of the engineering, construction and IT labour markets for professionals. The project will have the following benefits:

- Better understanding of the labour market experiences and needs of older professionals and modelling of the engineering, construction and IT labour markets.
- Understanding of the development and management of programmes targeting the training of mature-age professionals.
- Materials to help older workers manage their career and avoid redundancy.
- Materials and advice for employers.
- Trainees obtain new skills.
- Increased number of people with IT skills in the labour market and fewer redundancies among the target group.
- IT industry benefits from recruits with project management and industry experience.

Additionally, CamProf and OUBS are collaborating on the development of new project proposals, based on findings from the PIMOS project in collaboration with EIPOS and one of the Belgian partners.

Germany

As a result of the PIMOS project, EIPOS established a revised system of training courses adapted to the needs of older, experienced professionals to maintain their employability. It adjusted its training courses and methods of delivery as follows:

- New modules include sales management, staff management, environmental management, quality management, security management, financial management and communication skills.

- Increased accessibility of courses (eg more part-time and weekend courses for those in employment).
- Improved marketing of courses through a better understanding of the market.

The training courses follow a design model that connects knowledge acquisition and active behaviour of the participants. The training course runs parallel to the job. The time expenditure for the courses amounts to between 100 and 400 hours, depending on the course. Private study is supported by study materials and, in particular, multimedia.

Belgium

VION proposed to a major client a programme for its older technical staff, which has been taken up and is proving very successful. The innovative course is designed to broaden participants' knowledge-base and role, and make them more flexible. VION is now considering offering similar courses to other clients.

Additionally, participation in the project has given VION greater insights into the problems facing older workers. It has been a discussion partner with several institutions that are working in this area: employers' federations, trade unions, universities, firms and employment agencies. Its role in the project has also encouraged VION to examine its own policies towards older workers. The project has also contributed to government policy making, with the recent approval of new measures targeting older workers. Finally, a joint press conference with the Flemish Employers' Federation about the results of the investigation in 1500 companies has helped to increase wider awareness of the issue.

Determinants of success

We identified a number of determinants of the undoubted success of the project. These were:

- EIPOS as project co-ordinator had a thorough understanding of the LEONARDO programme and contractual and funding arrangements which promoted confidence and trust among the partners.
- All the partners were experienced in working in partnership with collaborators from other countries and on European Union funded projects.
- The project brought together individuals from a wide range of backgrounds and with skills in different areas, which meant that knowledge sharing was encouraged and team members benefited from each others' expertise.
- The project was simple and flexible with no requirements to rigidly preserve identical methodologies and approaches in different countries.

- The use of consultants in both Belgium and the UK meant that the project was quickly resourced, without the partner organisations having to implement time-consuming and costly staff recruitment procedures.
- The project struck the right moment in the UK and the European Commission in particular, with the issue of older workers coming on to the wider political and social agenda.
- Regular meetings were essential – providing deadlines, promoting sharing of ideas, generating new ideas, encouraging continuing communication and future collaboration.
- Openness by contractor and partners led to trust.
- Use of a single language. The German partner suggested the use of English by the project team, which meant that meetings were efficient, there was no requirement for translation, plus maximum ease of dissemination.
- The small group of countries involved made communication and co-ordination easy, and meetings of the group more manageable.
- The cultural activities included in each international meeting were an essential part of building mutual communication, understanding and trust.
- All the partners were capable of delivering the outputs required of them.
- Each partner had a direct interest in the activities allocated to them.

Concluding comments

The PIMOS project has provided much needed evidence on the support needed by older workers if they are to maintain their employability. Additionally, each of the projects has resulted in national benefits, in terms of the development of new kinds of training initiative in each of the partner countries. This is particularly the case in the UK, with the development of the innovative MAP>IT series of projects that came directly out of the PIMOS project and which involves both CamProf and OUBS. More broadly, this project raised the profile of the issue of age and employment among employers and their representatives, and among professional groupings. In the case of the latter, we have evidence that there was relatively little knowledge of the issue prior to PIMOS.

At a time when policy-makers are placing increasing emphasis on 'active' labour market programmes and the notion of 'active' ageing is also coming to the fore in policy debates, the PIMOS project has been important in highlighting the need for the targeting of programmes on older workers. However, while identifying areas where remedial action is required, our study has also demonstrated that labour market barriers facing older workers are deeply ingrained and will require concerted and long-term efforts from governments, employers, trade unions and professional institutions if they are to be overcome.

Further information

Further details can be found on the PIMOS website
www.camprof.demon.co.uk/pimos/home.htm.

Acknowledgements

We are indebted to Uwe Reese for conceiving the PIMOS project and inviting
us to join, his support during all phases of this study and for contributing material for this chapter. We are also grateful to the individuals and organisations
who agreed to be interviewed as part of this research. Finally, we are grateful
for the additional assistance of Uwe Reese, Adrien Coucke and Vera Kellens in
preparing this chapter.

13   Re-naissance – a case study of a UK charity's experience of a European lifelong learning project

John Rotherham and Paul Twynam

How can a charity dedicated to improving the lives of people with learning disabilities benefit from 'lifelong learning', while preventing 'burn out' amongst its staff? And what are the benefits of sharing experiences between similar organisations from different countries? A European Union- (EU) funded project, Re-naissance, provided answers to both questions – while posing many more questions for the participants.

The Home Farm Trust (HFT) is a national charity based in Bristol providing residential and other services for people with learning disabilities. Established since 1962 HFT currently operates over 15 locations throughout England, with 1,000 employees and a turnover of £20m. Prior to the Re-naissance project the Trust had participated in two EU-funded projects, both focussed on users of HFT services, rather than employees. Some of the participating organisations were also in the Re-naissance project.

Becoming a partner in the European Re-naissance project

We came to the Re-naissance project in 1997 as a small human resources (HR) department within the Trust. Neither of us had previous experience of working in Europe or of EU funding. The project leader was TAU-groep, a Flemish umbrella organisation for nine learning disability services (originally founded by Franciscans) in and around Brussels. We had been invited to become partners in an existing project, and had no input into the project design, or its submission to the European Commission. Our involvement had come about through the networking activities of HFT's development director who, after agreeing the contract and attending the inaugural meetings, was to play no further active part in the project. The first few meetings, therefore, saw us trying hard to get up to speed with the project aims, the nature of the other partner organisations, and the budgets; reaching a shared understanding of the aims of the project, its structure, desired outcomes and the sheer logistics of making this thing work.

What was Re-naissance?

Re-naissance was a 3 year project, ending in 2000, with the overall aim of preventing 'burn out'[1] by encouraging lifelong learning amongst 'front-line workers'[2] in the social-care sector, particularly those who were longer serving employees with few formal qualifications.

Underpinning this were two fairly large assumptions. Firstly, that this group of workers were particularly prone to 'burn out', due to the demands of care work and the rapidly changing nature of the social-care sector. Secondly, that by encouraging lifelong learning in this group – to help them get the 'learning habit' – they would be more able to cope with the pace of change. This would avoid burn out and result in lower absenteeism and turnover in the workforce. As HR professionals we were aware of some research that supported each assumption (Felce *et al* 1997, Rose 1997) but also felt intuitively that expressing this as a causal link was an article of faith, rather than an established fact.

There were two objectives about outcomes for the project. First, to work transnationally to develop a number of 'products'[3] that would help bring about a lifelong learning practice amongst 'frontline workers'. Second, to incorporate these into an HR management approach that would influence HR professionals and senior management in partner and similar organisations.

How the Re-naissance project was organised

Funding came from the EU through the LEONARDO programme. The participants were drawn from six countries (Austria, Belgium, Netherlands, UK, Hungary and Spain).[4] The Spanish organisations only participated in an observer capacity due to a funding shortfall (the EU gave us less than we had asked for and the Spaniards volunteered to take the short straw). There was only one Hungarian organisation, a service provider; they also had limited involvement as it believed it had more to learn than it felt it could

---

[1]'Burn out' – exhaustion or, at least, depressed work effectiveness brought about by occupational stress.

[2]Front-line workers – a term used in the project to denote paid or unpaid workers on a basic grade and working directly with the client group with learning disabilities.

[3]For the purposes of EC funding a 'product' is anything that was developed or produced during, or as a result of, the project. 'Products' from Re-naissance include: coaching training courses; journal articles; training evaluation methods; and descriptions of initiatives, such as learning accounts.

[4]*From Austria*: Institut für Sozialdienste Akademie für Sozialarbeit, Akademie für Sozialarbeit. *From Belgium*: TAU-groep, Vormingsleergang voor Sociaal en Pedagogisch Werk (VLOD), Kortrijk *From Spain*: Paz y Bien, Aprose. *From Hungary*: Összefogás Ipari Szövetkezet. *From the Netherlands*: Pameijer Keerkring, Nederlands Instituut voor Zorg en Welzijn (NIZW). *From the United Kingdom*: The Home Farm Trust (HFT), Norah Fry Research Centre.

contribute.[1] Theirs was also, regrettably, the only organisation where few employees spoke English – the agreed operating language.

In each of the four main participating countries, Hungary and Spain aside, there were two main partners. In each case, one was a provider of services for people with learning disabilities and the second an academic institution specialising in social care. HFT's UK partner was the Norah Fry Research Centre.[2] One of the first things we discovered was that our overseas partners generally had a closer relationship with academic institutes than we did. These 'pedagogic' institutes had a significant role in short-course training, as well as in courses of qualifying studies.

Additionally, the project brief required each country to involve front-line workers who were to participate actively in the project and be the 'subjects' and beneficiaries of it. This was to prove difficult as employees were reluctant to be identified with a group prone to 'burn out' and at least one of the products of the transnational work-groups floundered because the target group rejected the 'burnt out' label. The intention of involving all parties in the project was to prove unrealistic with front-line workers proving relatively uninterested in what were fairly dry discussions about HR management theory and techniques. The use of English as the operating language of the project also excluded them from the discussions more than the more 'senior' participants. By the run up to the final conference in October 2000, it had become evident to everyone that the project had evolved into one firmly focussed on HR practitioners and management. Front-line worker participation in the process of the project had become limited to the evaluation of products produced and indirectly, hopefully, as beneficiaries of what their employers had learned.

The project was structured around a series of transnational meetings. Each partner country hosted these in turn, except Spain. Over the 3 year period there were three 'working group' meetings of about 60 participants, including the front-line workers. Interspersed with these were six 'project group' meetings of the lead person from each country (six persons in total). The Brussels conference replaced the final transnational meeting and was designed to disseminate the project's products. A CD ROM of articles and products from the project were available to conference delegates. Additional copies of the CD are available, in the UK, through HFT.

---

[1]Hungary is not yet an EU member but has applied to join and is associated formally with the EU.

[2]The Norah Fry Research Centre was established in 1988 as part of the University of Bristol's Department of Mental Health. Its principal interests are the evaluation and development of services for people with learning difficulties. This is one of the leading centres in the UK for research into services for people with learning difficulties. Rigorous research conducted at the Centre evaluates services: highlighting good and innovative practice; identifying weaknesses; and suggesting areas for development.

First reactions to being involved in a European project

We started our involvement in Re-naissance with our own ideas about life-long learning, but little experience of Europe or of co-operative projects. We faced a project aim that we would have understood better if we had been able to read it in its Flemish original. The project had been born from the desire, initially and principally amongst the Belgians and Dutch, to have a project in the social-care sector that addressed the problems of their front-line workers.

The project seemed complex from the start. The structure of the project, its organisational logistics and the number of aims and agendas, sometimes conflicting, made us at worst sceptical and, at best uncertain, as to the eventual outcome. We were uncertain how our involvement in the project would directly benefit HFT and, more importantly, how it might indirectly benefit, or even disbenefit, HFT's clients.

HFT had committed us to the project and as individuals we were interested and hopeful but the project, in the first year even, seemed to lack tangible content. It was *all* 'process': the process of learning to work together, the process of forging the 'real' project out of the words that had been given to the Commission. We had still to create any substantive content.

During the 3 years of the project the aims were redefined, and the focus narrowed to an extent that the project's initial ambitions were achievable within the timescale. Crucial to the success and relevancy of Re-naissance for HFT was ensuring that the project aims fitted within the evolving learning and development strategy of our own organisation.

Questions of meaning – overcoming the barrier of language

In these circumstances, it took some time for us to feel fully involved, to get to know the other project members as individuals and to understand each other's work. It was only in the second or even third year that some of the conversations from the first year made complete sense. This was because of the inherent differences in the training and education institutions and paradigms of the member countries, and the misleading ease with which we spoke each other's languages (correction: the misleading ease with which they all spoke each other's languages, and with which all of them spoke English). English was our (unofficial) common language. However, we also heard a lot of Flemish and Dutch, which are dialects one of the other, and German, the sole language of many of the Austrians and, after Russian, the third language of some of the Hungarians.

Central to the project was the necessity to reach agreement on shared meaning. We shared many aspects of each other's culture, had shared experiences (of work, home, disability, and so on) and, through our work for people with disabilities, shared many values. Even so, terms such as 'lifelong learning' did not seamlessly transpose to the different organisations and cultures.

As an example, the Belgians wanted to start an initiative about self-steering teams. They introduced the experiment they were running within their organisation early on in the project and circulated written descriptions of its progress. But it was only at the beginning of the third year, at a meeting in Austria, that the nature of the experiment and the reason for the problems they were reporting became clear to us. The ability to listen to them face-to-face at a meeting was more important than we had realised. We needed to question them and to doggedly extract understanding from behind the barrier of familiar words borrowed to explain unfamiliar concepts. Time and again we heard people use an everyday English word only to discover, sooner *or later*, that they meant something quite different. At the end we had to compile a glossary to accompany the final conference proceedings.

What we brought with us – HFT's work on learning

At the start of Re-naissance, in 1997, we had just defined our own challenge: to take the organisation away from a 'training' paradigm towards 'learning'. The initial challenge once the project had begun, was to find a working definition of the rather slippery term 'lifelong learning'.[1] More difficult still was to find practical examples of what an organisation could do to encourage lifelong learning.

There was plenty of information relating to visionary educational and massive infrastructure projects. Apart from employee development and assistance programmes such as the famous Ford Motor Company's EDAP initiative (Beattie 1997) – itself resource-intensive – little was available that was easily portable to a large charity organisation. There is also a huge amount written on the 'learning organisation'. Whilst there is significant overlap with lifelong learning, we thought the crucial difference was that the learning organisation is almost exclusively about organisational outcomes, whilst lifelong learning outcomes are more personal to the individual, and the benefit to the organisation is often tangential.

If agreeing on language and meaning was difficult, as a group we also found it hard to agree on shared definitions and methods. One of the early points of shared understanding was the production of a checklist of values or

---

[1] We liked the definition in Longworth, N. and Davies, K.W. *Lifelong Learning*, 1996: 'Lifelong learning is: the development of human potential through a continuously supportive process which stimulates and empowers individuals to acquire all the knowledge, values, skills and understanding they will require throughout their lifetimes and apply them with confidence, creativity and enjoyment in all roles, circumstances and environments.'

'slogans' (below). We all subscribed to them, even though interpretations of them differed, as did the theory that informed them. Within HFT, our approach to these slogans was theoretically complemented by Howard Gardner's work on multiple intelligence theory (Gardner 1993), neuro-linguistic programming (O'Connor and Seymour 1995), accelerated learning (Rose 1985) and Tony Buzan's mind-mapping (Buzan 1993). For others, the theories underpinning the values were quite different. For example, the Dutch service provider, Pameijer-Keerkring, placed a lot of value on the work of Joseph Kessels, of Leiden University, on learning and a 'corporate curriculum'.

What was important for us was that these approaches could be incorporated into training practice, to create the conditions and act as a catalyst for change to bring about a culture of lifelong leaning in HFT. It is a paradox that we needed to use the structure of the traditional 'training course' (as well as other methods) in order to give away that control and empower employees to become lifelong learners.

We worked, both transnationally and within HFT, on coaching skills models and training courses for coaching skills. This was to move the training experience, both literally and metaphorically, closer to the employee. We also hoped that coaching would increase the likelihood of transference, through proximity to the on-the-job experience and by tailoring to individual need.

The other method we used to encourage employees into a learning culture was the introduction of HFT individual learning accounts (ILAs) for the front-line workers participating in the Re-naissance project, (Donaldson 1996).

Re-naissance - Our shared values about learning

- Access different learning styles – simultaneously!
- Build in reflection time on what is learnt – for the individual – for the team – for the organisation
- Encourage risk taking – for the trainer and participants
- Actively involve participants
- Encourage the use of coaching and mentoring techniques
- Give participants control of the learning process
- Link learning to organisational continuous improvement
- Develop individual learning plans/learning logs
- Keep learning close to the job experience
- Use the internal resources of the participant group
- Learn from failure – don't punish it
- Be a role model – highlight 'non-traditional' learning experiences
- Incorporate learning about learning in trainings
- Identify the learning moments in the working day
- Let the participants and the final target group (clients) evaluate the training in form and content.

This helped reconcile the inevitable tension between corporate training imperatives and individual developmental aspirations, whilst retaining clarity about the relative costs in the 'training budget'.

The eight front-line workers involved in Re-naissance were from HFT's scheme in Frocester, Gloucestershire, some 30 miles from the Trust's main office where the human resources department is based. They were encouraged to form a learning-support group and each was allocated £100 each year to spend on their own learning. We used the same name, 'individual learning accounts', for this arrangement as the UK Government did for a scheme of its own 2 years later. Each individual could choose to spend their ILA (which was in addition to any training and development budget that the scheme manager had at her disposal) on whatever they chose, so long as they expected to learn something from it and it did not represent the purchase of capital items.

The ILAs were spent on a variety of things. The subjects covered driving lessons, guitar tuition, swimming classes, a watercolour course, yoga classes, a conversational French course, a computer course, a Reiki healing course, and so on. The main purpose was to encourage use of the individuals' 'training muscles'. For organisations like HFT, the 'life-skills' and interests of employees contribute directly to the development and support of service users. For them, the ILA model has a shorter feedback loop into organisational benefits than in manufacturing organisations like Ford (Beattie 1997). The skills the Frocester front-line workers learnt were all directly transferable into work-based activities with service users.

The ILAs were probably the part of the project that they were most enthused by, not only by their relative novelty, but also by the control it gave them over their own development. Some participants have now continued, on their own, the activities they began with HFT support and funding.

Inclusion, contact and ownership – perceptions of a project

In retrospect we can say with some certainty and precision what the project outcomes and benefits were, and we will enumerate these later in this chapter. But at the start we couldn't, or didn't do this, and within the Trust we suffered some criticism as a result. Even now, our departmental colleagues who were not involved in the project ask 'When will it be our turn?'

When budgets are tight, as they must be in a charity, people will always query 'Who's paying for your trip to Rotterdam, then?' The perception of European 'jollies' had to be dispelled. Being able to report tangible benefits to the Trust at the end of the project has been an absolute prerequisite for involvement in subsequent ones. Like all training and development activities, mere faith in their effectiveness is not a sufficient substitute for a rigorous evaluation process.

Whilst the Frocester group were enthusiastic participants in ILAs, at another level they were guinea pigs for the project and its products. Thus, two of them attended one of the working-group meetings over 2 days in Rotterdam during the first year; during the third year another two went to Austria. But this degree of contact was too little and too infrequent. The physical distance of the scheme from Bristol also contributed to the relative isolation of this group. They never seemed to become an integral part of the project and, we suspect, never felt full ownership or involvement in it.

The lack of face-to-face contact had a significant braking effect on the project. We would return from the fairly short but intense overseas meetings fired with enthusiasm for the project and its end products, which we had been working on. Then real life took over, the in-tray had piled up and Re-naissance was put on hold. Weeks later we would get emails reminding us of some project deadline or other and would realise that we had done next to nothing since landing at the airport.

All Re-naissance partners had email and the TAU-groep devoted part of their website (see *European resources or the web* at end of this book) to the project. The site had public areas and areas accessible only to project members where minutes etc were posted. This technology was expected to solve the contact issue but, in truth, it was only marginally helpful. We did not have access to teleconferencing, so do not know if virtual meetings might have been a better compromise. We still feel, though, that there is no substitute for face-to-face contact.

For the Trust, part of the solution involved submitting another project bid to the UK LEONARDO Agency. This was for a trainer-exchange project, which we called Excel. The bid was successful in gaining funding for two people to each spend 2 weeks in the Netherlands and 2 weeks in Hungary. This prolonged contact made it much easier to examine and share concepts and techniques. In hindsight, it would have been beneficial to have that degree of face-to-face contact earlier in the larger Re-naissance project.

Looking back, it is blindingly obvious that the project was always going to be about the process of working together as much as it was going to be about lifelong learning, or 'burn out', or HR management. Certainly, the evidence of the Re-naissance products disguises the amount we learned about each other and ourselves from the project process. The project evolved and matured over its 3 year life span. The aims and direction developed, and each partner made them his or her own. Each contributed something and each took away something.

What we learned from Re-naissance – expected and unexpected

The most obvious area of learning for us came from the cross-cultural aspects of the project. This outcome wasn't uppermost in our minds when we started but, we reminded ourselves, it is one of the explicit aims behind the EU funding for all such projects. We had glimpses of everyday life in different countries: how the Budapest metro differs from its Rotterdam counterpart, what Austrian clothes shops look like, the difference between a Bristol pub and a bar in Brussels. We had opportunities to learn about 'higher culture' through museums, architecture and music, as well as many chances to sample unfamiliar food and drink. This taught us to notice the differences, whilst appreciating the many similarities.

In language too there were tantalising similarities and frustrating differences. In Bristol, an Austrian tried to explain what he wanted to drink to a Belgian. They thought that the German and Flemish words were very similar until the barman served the Belgian with apple juice instead of cider. We also found many proverbs that translated exactly from one language to another, presumably because they predated the migration of Anglo-Saxons to Britain, or the split between Dutch and 'Deutsch'.

More central to the project's aims was the exchange of ideas, models and techniques with other trainers and care professionals. For example, we were familiar with the work of John O'Brien, a Canadian, in the learning disability field, but it took a Dutch trainer running a workshop in Hungary to show us O'Brien's path-planning technique (Pearpoint *et al* 1995). This technique became one of the Re-naissance products and we have since used it in the Trust's management training and in organisational development work in our own department.

Coming from different organisations (and being from the same country did not necessarily help you understand another partner organisation) we were also confronted with the variety of ways in which roles within learning, training, development and education were divided. The relationship between trainers and line-managers varied greatly. Who owned and controlled the learning experience in the UK (a trio of the learner, the budget-holding manager and the 'expert' trainer) was different from the situation in the Netherlands (a quartet of the learner, their team manager, their team guide and a trainer). In Hungary, the Összefogás organisation has no trainers, in Belgium the trainers are mostly social workers, and in the Netherlands there is an individual called an orthopedagoog,[1] a profession that bears no relation to any occupational group we have in the UK.

In most of the continental countries, service providers recruit people with qualifications obtained from high schools (specialist vocational higher education institutions) and look to those same high schools or to universities for in-service education and training. In the Netherlands, the trainers in the service

---

[1] An orthopedagoog is, as far as we have gleaned, an individual who advises, as a technical expert, on learning disabilities those who are caring for these people. They are distinct and different from psychologists, social workers and psychiatrists.

provider organisation were contracted out to a University to deliver training to other service-provider organisations. In the UK, it is only recently that the FE and HE sector has become commercial and entered the training market. We were not used to these sorts of relationships, which were traditional elsewhere.

We also noticed that many of the partner organisations seemed more hierarchical than the Trust. The offices that we visited seemed more formal, relationships between managers and the managed were more reserved or detached. Concomitantly, we gained the impression that many of the front-line workers were less autonomous than their English counterparts. All this is, of course, on the basis of a very small sample of each country's care sector, but it had to be taken into account when developing the project.

Every organisation we came into contact with had the care of its clients as its central purpose, and we felt that all the people we met worked hard and put effort into their work. We did, however, see behaviour that suggested that the work/life balance in the UK is somewhat different from elsewhere. A good example of this is the occasion when the project co-ordinator asked at a meeting what everyone's holiday plans were for the coming year. Everyone reeled off the weeks or months that they were taking as leave until it came to us. We had no idea when we were going on holiday next year, but knew that, when we did go, it would be at short notice and for nowhere near as long as our European colleagues. We exhibited surprise that they could know so far in advance what they were doing and they were totally amazed that we didn't. Somehow, we felt they had things in better perspective than we did.

Discussing care and training practice within the project also meant that we had to understand the different national contexts for our work: the legal framework, funding arrangements, the national education system, the organisation of professions, models for care, etc. It is difficult to say what we learned from this that could usefully be transferred to the UK context, so much was a product of the different historical traditions, political alliances, the distribution of power between local and national government etc.

One difficulty this all raised was when we came to advise the Hungarian organisation. As we have said, Hungary is waiting to become a full member state of the EU and has a lot of leeway to make up, coming from their country's recent past as part of the Warsaw Pact. All their national institutions, paradigms, models of best practice, etc, are being turned on their head or else don't exist at all. The Hungarian service provider, Összefogás, needs help with very basic HR practice, training and development, and organisational development. They asked all the project partners for help. However, they have received advice from partners whose HR and care practice is rooted in different traditions. If Összefogás managed to synergise this into a coherent whole they will have done a magnificent job and may reap the true 'synergy benefits', on the other hand, they may end up with an ill-fitting patchwork that doesn't work.

One of the most profound learning experiences comes from the cross-cultural, multilingual aspect of the project that we have already mentioned. But this time it is an entirely inward reflective style of learning; having to express yourself in English is a test. Even when English is your native language or perhaps *because* it is your native language, you have to modify it when you are talking with someone for whom it is a second language, no matter how fluent they are. Firstly, you have to take out all the slang, dialect, cultural references and much of the humour, at least until you know the individual rather well. Secondly, you also have to be careful about pronunciation and monitor much more closely the verbal and non-verbal feedback you are getting from the other person. Thirdly, you have to explain your concepts in simple language without using any jargon and without assuming that you share a common understanding of any complex concepts.

One result is that you 'install' a language monitor between brain and tongue (which continues to operate for some days after returning to the UK). The other, more profound outcome, is that you find that you have rigorously examined your understanding of your own work, have had to dissect the assumptions that you usually work on, and had to justify the reasons for most of the things you usually do without any thought.

The final part of the learning that resulted from the project is the content of the project products themselves. These are better studied in their complete form in the Re-naissance Conference Pack/CD. But, for the record, the outcomes of the project include:

- A training evaluation methodology (UK and Netherlands);
- A report on involving clients with learning disabilities in the evaluation process (UK);
- Various coaching skills courses (UK and Netherlands);
- Coaching, project work and self-steering team initiatives (Belgium);
- Refreshment (a 'time-out' stress alleviation intervention from Austria);
- Path planning (the Netherlands);
- Individual learning accounts (UK);
- A lifelong learning/learning organisation, 'corporate curriculum' checklist (UK and the Netherlands).

Conclusion

'Would we do it again?' Well, we would do it differently, but the overall experience has been a positive one, with lots of work, new colleagues and friends, and a willingness to build on the links and work together in the future. Hindsight has taught us some lessons:

- Get in at the start – influence the project submission;
- Leave your assumptions at the door and check them at every turn;

- Prepare to compromise;
- Be prepared for different working styles (eg attitude to time and deadlines);
- Tell 'the folks back home' what's going on (internal PR);
- Synchronise European project aims with local organisational strategy;
- Work at communication – face-to-face with partners and using electronic means;
- Look for opportunities to make wider connections between organisations;
- Keep a continually open mind about what you can learn AND contribute;
- Have fun.

References

Beattie, A. (1997) *Working People and Lifelong Learning: A Study of the Impact of an Employee Development Scheme*, NIACE

Buzan, T. (1993) *The Mind Map Book*, BBC Books

Donaldson, L. (1996) 'Encouraging the learning habit at Oxford Brookes', *IRS Employment Review: Employee Development Bulletin,* 76, 13–15

Felce, D., Harris, P., Hatton, C., *et al* (1997) *Staff in Housing Services for People with Learning Disabilities: Stress, Support, Training and Selection*, Welsh Centre for Learning Disabilities Applied Research Unit and Welsh Division of the British Institute of Learning Disabilities

Gardner, H. (1993) *Multiple Intelligences: The Theory in Practice*, Basic Books

Home Farm Trust www.hft.org.uk

Kessels, J.W.M. (2000) *Learning, the Corporate Curriculum and Knowledge Productivity,* Keynote Address, 'Towards a Learning Society', Portuguese EU Presidency, Lisbon 28–30 May 2000

Longworth, N. and Davies, K.W. (1996) *Lifelong Learning*, Kogan Page

Norah Fry Research Centre www.bris.ac.uk/Depts/NorahFry

O'Connor, J. and Seymour, J. (1995) *Introducing Neuro-Linguistic Programming: Psychological skills for understanding and influencing people*, HarperCollins

Pearpoint, J., O'Brien, J. and Forest, M. (1995) *Path: A Workbook for Planning Positive Possible Futures* (2nd edition), Inclusion Press

Re-naissance Project www.taugroep.be/renaissance.htm

Rose, C. (1985) *Accelerated Learning*, Accelerated Learning Systems Ltd

Rose, J. (1997) 'Stress and stress management among residential care staff', *Tizard Learning Disability Review,* 2 (1), 8–15

14 CICERO: a journey into Europe

Frances Homewood

Setting off

As ever, the simplest ideas are the most effective. The idea behind this citizenship/adult learning initiative was to open up access to Europe for people from very marginalised communities, in a way that would be useful and meaningful to them. What better way than to actually go there?

This was the thinking that informed the bid, in 1996, European Year of Lifelong Learning, for monies to run a pilot project. The idea evolved from work done by the South Yorkshire District of the Workers Educational Association (WEA), in which they had taken a group of students and tutors from the coalfields area on a long bus journey to Strasbourg (Hartley 1997). Neither 'capacity building' nor 'citizenship' were fashionable words at that time, yet the effects of the policies destroying Yorkshire communities demanded an appropriate response. Learning, in all shapes and forms, was one such response. The value of study visits in opening darkened horizons and creating new forms of confidence was an invaluable tool.

The aim of the new initiative, developed in 1996 and implemented by a small steering group of experienced adult education practitioners, was twofold. Firstly, we aimed to bring together people from a number of communities facing similar problems, give them a short but intensive briefing on the workings of the European Union (EU) institutions and decision-making structures, and then provide the opportunity to see at first-hand what happens in Brussels. This enhanced the initial work, in that it opened up the networking possibilities across communities; people learning from each other's rich experiences.

The second aim was to explore the notion of citizenship within a European context. The European Commission and Parliament were increasingly concerned about the remoteness of their operations from those they were meant to be serving, particularly on the social agenda. The Eurosceptic media, and an unco-operative British government, had exacerbated an inherent structural weakness to the point where Brussels officials felt completely invisible to British citizens in a way unparalleled in other member states. And on the part of the citizen, particularly those facing poverty and exclusion, there was the evidence of vast resources available from Brussels, together with an increasing number of decisions emanating from the Euro centre, and yet a yawning gap in understanding how it all worked. The very sophisticated levels of knowledge required seemed to belong to very few, most of whom were professionals.

If it was possible therefore to engage more with debates happening in other member states, where the notion of European citizenship was much more on the agenda, this could be an important, relevant and useful tool in building the capacity of marginalised communities. It was, of course, essential to do this from a critical perspective. The journey must be started with an open mind as to how far the European model could offer social inclusion in the UK when there was clear evidence of its xenophobic and racist tendencies.

The journey

In October 1996, the project organisers approached several centres known for their innovative approaches to adult learning, and invited them to recruit unemployed activists to the pilot project. Those involved in the project were:

- Castleford Women's Centre, born from the aspirations of miners' wives to have education for life after the 1994 strike, who accepted the invitation with alacrity.
- The Dearne Valley WEA branch.
- In Liverpool, local community workers had strong links with unemployed activists who were keen to take up the learning opportunity.
- A link with Northern Ireland was established through the Women into Politics organisation, who had a track record of working across the sectarian divide.
- Thomas Danby College in Leeds, serving the mainly African Caribbean communities of Chapeltown was invited to participate.
- The more traditional Ruskin and Fircroft Colleges, whose Return to Learn Courses had built the confidence of many disaffected adults, were also invited.

In all, 42 participants were invited to an initial residential course at Northern College, Barnsley. We called on the European expertise of tutor Jane Pillinger to introduce the workings of the EU and the roles of the various institutions. The questions of 'What has this got to do with us?' and 'How can we influence it to the benefit of our community?' were central to the process. As ever, the thrill of meeting people from diverse, unknown, yet strangely familiar communities gave the atmosphere its edge. The residential was an important first stage for the subsequent 5 days in Brussels.

As project co-ordinator I felt slightly awed at leading this group across the water, knowing that for many it would be their first trip abroad and required tremendous courage. One enduring memory is of seeing Agnes, flanked by her mates, stepping onto a London Underground escalator after many years confined at home in her white working-class community with agoraphobia. I was even more moved when she later told me that it was on this trip that she'd had her first conversation with a black British person.

In recognising my own lack of awareness of the European scene, however, I felt at one with the group. We were all carrying in our baggage the myths and stereotypes of the British press. I too felt grateful for the chance to judge for myself.

The study visit programme, spanning 5 days, combined meetings with politicians and policymakers in the Commission with, most importantly, meetings with local groups facing diverse forms of exclusion. These two dimensions proved to be crucial. It was only from our dialogue with the Conseil des Communautés Africaines de Belgique that we were able to discuss in the Parliament the forms of discrimination that it had not tackled in relation to migrant workers in the EU. Visits to the Marolle, the impoverished heart of Brussels, saved from the developers bulldozers by the collective actions of its residents in the 1970s, resonated with group members active in tenants' struggles in the north of England. And discussions on employment strategies in the Commission were informed by the knowledge of impressive Flemish childcare facilities available to working parents in some parts of the city. The highlight of the visit for many was the encouraging message from Structural Funds Director Graham Meadows, who placed the responsibility for regeneration back in the communities, but pledged practical and direct support for grassroots initiatives.

The outcomes of the 'pilot' were threefold. First, and most evident, was a remarkable increase in confidence on the part of participants. Simply from this brief experience, we heard reports of people getting back into work for the first time in years, pursuing further and higher education, developing new aspirations. Secondly, there was an impact on the organisations back in the community. New funding opportunities that had been identified in Brussels were followed up, and the 'buzz' from the visit seemed to spread so that, thirdly, the pilot group were keen to extend to others the opportunity they'd had. They also had a thirst for more Euro learning that they felt would best be done through the informal network which had been created. Hence, CICERO; Community Initiatives in Citizenship Education Regionally Organised, was born.

Travelling together

Participants in the 'pilot' project then established a steering group, with the aim of getting future resources and widening the network. The issue was how such a learning programme around Europe, including the crucial element of travel, could be funded without getting embroiled in complicated transnational partnerships. The steering group was clear that it wanted the programme to be accessible to grassroots activists, and provide the missing link of understanding and access without which they would always be beholden to European 'experts'. In particular, money for childcare and subsistence was essential.

What emerged from the discussions was an idea of a longer, more comprehensive learning programme that would put local issues in a European context, and give activists the skills and confidence they wanted. It would include a Brussels visit and, in order to attract the funding available for Capacity Building and increasing employability, would be accredited. Thanks to contacts with an enlightened official from the Government Office for Yorkshire and Humberside, who was impressed by the results of the 'pilot', European funding was secured. As ever, the match funding was the stumbling block and it took almost a year before the DfEE (now the DfES) was persuaded that some of their funds aimed at widening participation could justifiably be used.

Somewhat daunted by the task of developing the learning materials, getting them accredited through the Open College Network (OCN), recruiting 50 participants, briefing local tutors and setting up the appropriate administrative systems, the steering group and co-ordinator worked long and hard to be ready for the new programme to start in January 1998. There were no models; innovation has its drawbacks and, without the moral and practical support of the partners, especially the WEA, the project would have failed

But the energy released from that first Brussels visit seemed to continue. Fifty new participants, now to be called 'community animateurs', to reflect the European flavour, were recruited. The programme devised covers 1 year and consists of five modules: Europe, Democracy and Citizenship; How Europe Works; Making it Work for Us; Brussels Study Visit; Finding Funding; and Social Exclusion. Each module lasts 10 weeks and consists of 3 hours 'contact' time, with another 3 hours private study/research time per week. The modules were accredited at levels 2 and 3 of the OCN framework (a more introductory level, one element, was added later). The last two modules were developed as a direct result of the participation of activists on the group developing the curriculum.

Participants included those from the 'pilot' and from new areas that were approached and engaged. These were, Nottingham Partnership Council, an inner city estate in Bradford, and more ex-mining communities in South Yorkshire. All participants had to fulfil the criteria of being unwaged or in part-time, casual employment and, in addition, be active in some way in their communities. Priority was given to those without post-school qualifications.

The two residential modules during the year proved crucial in building confidence, linking communities and sharing experiences. This process continued in the ferry journeys, late-night singing sessions and heated discussions of the study visits. Differences in geography, ethnicity, faith and experience brought up difficulties that were not always resolved.

There were some magical moments; watching three animateurs hold a group of Commission officials working on citizenship issues spellbound with accounts of their lives in inner city, black, or mining communities. 'People were genuinely moved and enthralled by the meeting,' said the letter that acknowledged the value of this two-way dialogue. The first annual conference, organised by volunteers, in which well-informed workshops were led by working class animateurs confident in European issues, was inspiring.

Equally, some groups became dysfunctional. The pressures of 'exclusion' showed themselves in a variety of ways; at least two participants' alcohol addiction became evident; other mental illness emerged. One of the groups broke down because of conflict around race issues. There were some important lessons to be learnt and changes to be made before starting the second round of recruitment in 1999.

The steering group spawned new sub-groups to develop appropriate policy on a range of issues, all of which drew on the expertise of animateurs who became increasingly involved in running the organisation. One key change was the size of each animateur group; increased from five to a minimum of ten participants. The selection criteria of being unemployed or in low waged, part time employment without higher educational qualifications remained. But there was more emphasis on ensuring that animateurs were currently active in their communities, and thus able to disseminate what they had learnt.

Another significant change involved the revision of the curriculum. The learning materials were radically re-written, feedback having shown that they started from too abstract a notion of democracy and citizenship. They became more focussed on self, locality, community. And the study visit was moved to the end of the programme, to maximise the benefits and knowledge arising from it.

The project itself also had to mature to deal with the increased numbers of people and regions involved. It took on Limited Company status and struggled with how to make the new Board of Trustees regionally representative and democratically accountable to its members. Fierce debates about the meaning of 'regionally organised' in our title reflected this struggle to be inclusive, whilst expanding into new areas at a rapid pace. Groups established in South Wales and Belfast brought up communication and accessibility issues to an organisation still Yorkshire dominated.

The reputation of the work grew, both in Brussels and with the funders. A substantial National Lottery grant allowed the appointment of new staff. We made a conscious effort to employ some of the animateurs who had helped shape the organisation. By the end of 1999 we were in a position to create a team, with DfEE backing, which could run a series of dissemination events around the country, presenting the CICERO model as an innovative and effective capacity building tool in marginalised communities. By the end of April 2000 another 130 participants from ten different communities had completed the programme, bringing the total to over 200 CICERO animateurs.

The view from here

If there are lessons to be drawn that are applicable to other ventures – the 'if' being acknowledgement of how local or small initiatives must be responsive to local situations, which will be historically specific – then they must be around two issues. The first is that of not under-estimating the sheer scale of the process we call 'capacity building', or 'widening participation'. The personal and collective journey on which people embark is vast. They, and the organisation and individuals who support them, need a lot of resources – physical, financial, and spiritual. In CICERO there were extraordinary outcomes; many described their lives as changed. There were also people; animateurs, tutors, organisers who got defeated by the process and the commitment required. If the Learning and Skills Councils and the providers are to really embrace such initiatives they will need to recognise the small results as well as the large, the subtle progress as well as the obvious.

The second lesson is that if there is an idea that is visionary and which gives people the chance to do what most of us love, ie to travel and to learn, the possibilities are transformative. Travellers have long known that when they take themselves away from what is familiar it is both challenging and expansive. They come back with new perspectives on what was familiar, and can see in new ways its potential for change. This is an essential experience for the animateur. A recently published OECD report told us that communities are becoming 'hyper mobile' and thus in danger of further breaking down. This is not so if you are poor; the reverse – the isolation born of no resources to travel and to learn, is a bigger danger. As one animateur put it, 'I've now seen what unemployment is like in other countries; I'm going to do something about it here'.

References

Hartley, T. (1997) 'Bonjour Citoyen', *Adults Learning*, 8(4)
Further details are available on the CICERO website: www.ciceroproject.org

Section IV
Changing policies and institutions

15　Benefitting from European activities in a college of further education

Lisa Morris

Introduction

As a late 'incomer' to the further education (FE) sector, after 15 years in local Government, I feel I can still offer an objective perspective on the role and influence of the FE sector in promoting the European dimension within life-long learning. I am always disappointed in the lack of recognition that the FE sector receives for its innovative work in promoting the European dimension to client groups, who include some of the hardest to reach target groups in society. The sector has also been at a major disadvantage in this work due to the complex methodology of its mainstream funding and the barriers this creates for the sector in promoting this vital activity; it remains to be seen how the Learning and Skills Council will affect this situation. My presentation is a very personal view, based on my own experience at Park Lane College and the many discussions I have had with colleagues from across the UK. I hope this, in some small way, recognises the work that is taking place within FE colleges.

Where did it all start?

In 1989 I took up the post of Lecturer in European Studies, a 2 year temporary contract moving from a permanent position that paid over £4,000 a year more than the post I was moving into. I am often asked why. The answers are simple:

- My current job as a local authority European Social Fund (ESF) Co-ordinator as far as I was concerned, was not 'European' enough. It relied heavily on my finance background and my line managers were not interested in expanding my role to explore the newly emerging and innovative education and training programmes from the European Commission (relevant for the first time outside of the higher education sector), or the new and innovative transnational structural funds initiatives, EURO-FORM, HORIZON and NOW.
- FE appealed to me because of the wide range of client groups it served – my particular interest being in the non-traditional student population. Park Lane College had already in 1989 expanded enormously into over 40 outreach sites throughout the inner city of Leeds, in some of the most

deprived wards in England. In my mind, FE in the UK was the first 'second chance school' option for many clients and, for me, it represented an opportunity to open up not just lifelong learning for all but the whole European dimension.

- Last but not least – it was a challenge!

The then principal of Park Lane College said to me, 'Prove that there is real value to Park Lane College in regard to the European dimension and the post will be re-assessed – but don't cost the college any money!' To minimise the cost to college I was given a 15 hour per week teaching programme, with remission hours to develop a European strategy for the college. Looking back, this particular principal was a 'rare beastie' in that he recognised that there was some potential for the FE sector to become more involved in pan-European activities, and took the risk of providing a resource (even if limited) to develop this. It is thanks to his vision and ability to take a limited risk so early on that the college now works with over 40 European partners across 17 European countries, with developing relationships and projects in South Africa, China and the Ukraine. The European Office is now the International Office, with 8.5 full time equivalent staff, managing and co-ordinating over 54 EU-funded projects – all transnational.

What did we do?

So how did the college get to this? It was not easy, and the first message to any colleague given this responsibility is 'don't be faint-hearted' and never accept the words 'no', 'not possible', 'not approved'. To survive you need to have enthusiasm, lots of energy, perseverance and very thick skin. Barriers do not just exist outside of the college – most barriers are internal – finance, fear and/ or total apathy. When I started at Park Lane College, I was seen as that 'mad woman', another of the principal's 'whims'. Other than a couple of long-standing French and German exchanges, there was no trans-European activity in place or being developed.

My first task was to find a person within a vocational area who could actually see and understand the real potential on offer, and who was willing to invest their time (outside of their normal hours) in supporting that belief by working with me. At Park Lane College I found this ray of sunshine and hope in the programme manager for Leisure, Travel and Tourism. She and I met and bonded in the belief that what was needed in this particular vocational area was real European work experience for the Leisure, Travel and Tourism students. How could these students possibly advise future customers on the best holiday and leisure activities in other European countries if they had not experienced this themselves? Then came PETRA, the Commission programme that supported the integration of the European dimension into vocational programmes. We sat and wrote the required two pages describing what our proposed 'pilot' project included, which was basically the development of a pan-European network through which we could develop and implement an accredited work experience module for Leisure, Travel and Tourism students. It was approved, and we were allocated 10,000 ECU for the first year to pull our network together in order to be able then to apply for a further 3 years funding!

The college's Leisure, Travel and Tourism programme is now totally trans-national, sending over 250 students per year on study visits, short-term and long-term placements to other European countries, including Poland. The college receives similar students from our partners to undertake similar activities in the UK. The majority of the students in these vocational areas are from inner city backgrounds, low achievers at school, many from disadvantaged families, lone parents, parents who are unemployed or have low incomes. Thanks to that acorn planted in 1990, they now undertake an NVQ in a foreign language or languages, have an accredited work placement in another country, and are virtually guaranteed a job on return. Employers have admitted that these students on return from their placements are their ideal future employees, due to their maturity, confidence, ability to work in teams, but also to work unsupervised, excellent communication and customer-care skills – all these skills truly developed while on their placements. Many students each year take up job offers in the country of their placement, France, Spain. Greece and Ireland being the most popular. However, one of the most surprising results has been when students seen as low achievers on entry to Park Lane College, realise their potential as confidence and self-esteem grow, and so move into higher education, an opportunity never considered by many of them when they first applied to Park Lane College.

Development in this vocational area did not stop here. The passion and the enthusiasm spread to other team members, which resulted in a further pilot project being submitted under the new LEONARDO programme to create a totally new vocational qualification recognising the emerging job profile of the 'animateur' – the member of staff in a hotel or leisure facility with responsi-bility for developing and implementing the activity schedule for all customers, regardless of age, sex, nationality or ability. Building on the initial PETRA network, a transnational partnership of eight countries set out to develop this new qualification, achieve pan-European accreditation and produce paper-based and multimedia material. The project was co-financed for 3 years, attracting 225,000 ECU under LEONARDO to support the additional costs of the total network. I don't think any of us at Park Lane College, or any one of the other European partners, expected the level of success finally achieved. The new programme is being delivered in England, Scotland, Finland, Greece, Spain and Belgium, with specialist modules being integrated into travel and tourism programmes in Denmark. Pan-European accreditation was achieved through the Institute of Travel and Tourism and use of an 'animateur' passport.

Paper-based training materials were written and translated into English, French, Spanish, Flemish and Italian, with a CD ROM – 'Animateur O' – being produced to test the knowledge of trainee animateurs, including their use of foreign languages. A lasting memory for me will be of all the partners sitting in a hotel lounge, on a dark, bleak Scottish January evening, writing multiple-choice questions for the CD ROM! The project has now been submitted for further funding to expand the network into 13 countries (22 partners), including Poland, Estonia and Hungary. Probably one of the most dramatic and unexpected results for Park Lane College from the animateur project is the close links with employers in Majorca. Not only are they employing our animateur graduates, but now come to Park Lane College to support the training activities, and interview both prospective employees and trainees for their summer placements.

Many readers will probably regard Leisure, Travel and Tourism as an easy option for integrating the European dimension into the curriculum. However, working with learners who have, in the main, left school not realising their full potential, not liking school, and certainly not wanting to learn a foreign language, is not an easy option at all. In addition, when you tell them that they could be undertaking 13 week placements in another country as part of their course, it is quite a daring challenge, particularly to those who have never left Leeds or Yorkshire before. It was this that captured the interest of the BBC in 1999 and resulted in a 30 min documentary being produced, following a group of our typical trainees on placement in Majorca.

Integrating the European dimension was as important for our adult population as for our young people. This population, as in many FE colleges, includes some of the most disadvantaged in our society, including people with disabilities (physical, sensory and learning), unemployed (particularly long-term unemployed), lone parents, non-UK ethnic origin, those without basic skills (particularly numeracy and literacy), ex-offenders, those recovering from drugs or alcohol abuse, the homeless, many with multiple disadvantage. With the support of the relevant directors at college, we were determined that these students should also benefit from the European dimension. In 1990 the college submitted three projects under the new Community Initiatives EUROFORM and HORIZON, which were approved for the period 1991–93 attracting over £1 million of ESF. What was exciting about these projects was that there had to be an element of transnationality, and so we worked with partners in Portugal (EUROFORM) and Greece (HORIZON).

The aim of the EUROFORM project was to attract adult returners into maths, sciences and IT. It was also the college's first taste in delivering training by telematics to single parents, or parents who could not leave the home. The transnational element with Portugal was exchanging experience with an escola in Portalegre, also developing IT training, so trainers were able to compare methodologies and approaches to learning. However, both partners were keen to exchange students, to provide them with an opportunity of experiencing the added value of the bilateral partnership. So, in 1992 and 1993, students undertook a 2 week work-based visit to Portalegre in the mountains of northern Portugal, a visit that included language and cultural training supported by cultural visits, visits to employers in Portalegre and joint IT training in the escola. Participants in both years included single parents, adults over 50 years of age, and the 'insecurely' housed, all having left school without adequate qualifications and unemployed at the start of the programme. The impact was dramatic. Tutors who accompanied these groups were astounded at what they learned about the learners – not realising how little they knew about them from the 2 years while at college. Somehow, in leaving Leeds and the UK many of them left their personal baggage behind, and began to communicate more effectively with each other and their tutors, developing self-help groups. The visit raised their own individual aspirations as new opportunities were identified, and personal confidence and self-esteem grew. The visits were not without their problems, which included, on one occasion, a late-night visit from the local police, but the final results outweighed these problems. Many of the participants went on to university as mature students, others directly into jobs. One student wrote to us from university stating that it was not until she had decided to do her final year thesis based on her study visit to Portugal that she realised the impact that this visit had, in terms of influencing her future (including her choice of future partner).

More broadly, the EUROFORM project had an enormous impact on Park Lane College as it had provided information technology as a tool. The college's IT strategy developed from this, and further Community Initiative bids were successful, helping the College in developing a telematics infrastructure, which not only targeted disadvantaged client groups, but also facilitated work-based learning for micro enterprises, so extending access to lifelong learning from non-traditional client groups. Funding under HORIZON (disadvantaged) from 1995 to 1997, followed by funding under INTEGRA (1998–2000) continued to pilot remote learning for disadvantaged client groups, and ADAPT (1998–2000) for small- and medium-sized enterprises (SMEs), targeting SMEs employing fewer than 50 people. The projects resulted in a college support centre being set up to tutor and administer new vocational programmes remotely using the telematics system called the **learning**line, widening participation in lifelong learning to both target groups. The new vocational programmes included a package accredited through West Yorkshire Open College Network (WYOCN), called quick skills, a series of stand-alone modules accredited at levels 2 and 3 providing IT, Business, Animal Care and Environment programmes. In addition, the underpinning knowledge for level 2 in customer care was rewritten for use on the **learning**line, as was an accredited career-development programme.

The system allows the client groups to learn at work, home or from a local centre, whenever they are able to give time to their own personal development. It can be accessed 24 hours per day, 365 days per year. Both the system and the quick skills modules were successfully piloted by partners in France and Spain, showing that the technical and pedagogical approach were also relevant in other countries. The unique features of the **learning**line is that it is easy to use by IT illiterate client groups, and quick skills offers learning in bite-size chunks, allowing learners to achieve in 15–20 mins, ie in lunch breaks, before starting work, or while the children are having naps!

The HORIZON projects of 1991–93 also continued through further HORIZON bids into 2000. These projects particularly focussed on people with disabilities. HORIZON (1991–93) recognised that not all the colleges students, particularly those with disabilities, would be able to participate in transnational visits and exchanges, but could become involved in programmes that promoted the European dimension. Under the OCN's Basic Skills Framework, the European Experience programme was developed to provide an insight into living and working in Europe for students with special needs, including French and German language tasters. Additional development took place in 1995–97, to incorporate knowledge of disabled people's rights in Europe, working with partners in France, Spain and Italy. This latter issue particularly focussed on barriers to employment in each country and how these barriers could be overcome. The final project, finishing in June 2000, continued to develop this theme, looking at the UK NVQ framework as a barrier and developing support materials to overcome this, but also exploring and developing new support structures, including specialist aids to overcome problems that dyslexia can create. This latter initiative was developed in conjunction with a newly found partner in Ireland, resulting in joint trainer workshops and seminars. In all these projects, transnational activities undertaken by the beneficiaries was seen as just as important as the exchange of trainers, experts and of knowledge. Students with physical disabilities visited Barcelona to evaluate the new public-access adaptations to roads and public transport, to support mobility for disabled people. Five 'homeless' beneficiaries visited Belgium and France, investigating issues of social exclusion, racism and xenophobia, as well as homelessness in other European countries. They also participated in a large international dissemination event in the European Parliament. Forty-seven women from Leeds, representing Park Lane College and many voluntary agencies, met with another 200 women from Spain, Italy, Denmark, Germany, France and Belgium in Ghent to celebrate International Women's Day, which again included a reception at the European Parliament.

The benefits are clear and should be made available to wider audiences across Europe. Listen to what our beneficiaries have to say:

In my opinion this work experience is a fantastic idea. Putting aside the social and cultural experiences, I think there is no better way to learn the French language than to experience it first hand by speaking the language all day. On my own I would never have dared to work in a large hotel, but I thought this excursion was well planned so I had no fears in giving it a go.   (Richard, France)

During my work experience in Spain I made friends with a lot of people. I also got to know people from other businesses around where we worked. Going to Spain gave me a lot of self confidence and when I got back I was more mature. I learned a lot of different skills which will help me a lot in this country. Overall it was a great experience and I really enjoyed it.   (Amajid, Spain)

I would seriously recommend continuing the LEONARDO programme for future young people because it helps you to see what there is on offer in other countries and it also brings the group of participants much closer together.   (Ghazanfar, Spain)

I had such a good time I am going back to Skibbereen next year and hopefully ask if I can work at Lissard as the place was so special and different from anything else I've seen or been to before. I loved every moment of it and felt I learnt a lot about outdoor conservation and the wildlife of Ireland. People need to take this chance and they may have doubts at first but it is the best thing I've ever done and hope that other people will feel the same.   (Gemma, Republic of Ireland)

Working within the social inclusion agenda has encouraged the college to work with other agencies from across the city, particularly schools and voluntary organisations. Involving them within the European dimension has also been an exciting journey for the college. The college is benefiting from these local partnerships, sharing its own experience of working internationally, as well as its transnational partners, to enable these organisations to participate. The confidence, experience and knowledge of working with partners in other countries is now paying off, as many of them have found their own transnational partners to work with, organisations more appropriate to their specific client groups.

   And what about staff development? The integration of the European dimension within lifelong learning is not restricted to our client groups. A transnational meeting can provide inflammatory passion and stimulus for an FE tutor. Staff, whether they are academic or administrative, feel the same 'buzz' or 'electricity' from participation in a transnational event – leaving behind local and national politics, the internal frustrations, lack of understanding, or recognition of the added value of the European dimension. To meet with like-minded people from other countries is better than the most miraculous tonic available in any country's health system. Lifelong learning need not be an accredited or nationally recognised achievement. Or is it only the effect of excellent local wines, camaraderie and good food? Let's learn from those who have participated in transnational activities:

> Working transnationally adds an element of excitement, spontaneity and chaos which I have found nowhere else in 30 years of employment! The added value of working with other nationalities, to other timetables and to other mindsets, is immeasurable – no 2 days are alike, the learning curve is always steep and continuous but the conclusions are satisfying and unlike working in any other area of expertise.
>
> (Carolyn Booth, Projects Officer, International Office)

> I have been fortunate to be able to use LEONARDO trainer placements to Spain (Mallorca) for the last three consecutive years and through this programme have developed some terrific links and made many great friends. By returning to the same country I have been able to expand our placement programme from 12 students in the first year to nearly 50 this year, as well as developing our taught programme in college. We have developed some superb training programmes and are able to offer placements to students from a wide range of courses in the college. Through the work done overseas I was approached by the BBC and last year worked with them profiling four of our Animation students working in Mallorca in the 'Close-Up North' documentary. The college has also been awarded 'Beacon College' status as a result of the development with the Animateur Programme which has grown from thought, some five years ago, to a nationally acclaimed qualification.
>
> (Jonathan Smith, Programme Manager for Travel and Tourism)

> Dealing with international partners has proved a great experience for me as a Work Experience Placement Officer. I have received the opportunity to meet my counterpart within a Polish school, a new group of prospective students in their home country, introduce them to the possibility of a work experience visit in my home town, and be part of their support team throughout the arrangements and visit. My initial attitude was 'would this exchange really work?' to a final attitude of 'I am looking forward to the next group of young people'. It was great to be caught up in their enthusiasm and to look at my own area through new eyes. It soon becomes apparent when working with other colleagues from similar establishments overseas that we all have similar aims and goals and we have far more in common with each other than we could have anticipated.   (Jan Wilkinson, Work Experience Officer)

> Communicating with people of different nationalities by email, fax and telephone adds a very interesting dimension to my job as clerk typist. I have learned that it is relatively easy to share a sense of humour even

when communication is limited by a language barrier. When I have been involved in transnational meetings I have been impressed by the value of trainers of different nationalities being able to share expertise and experiences, and also by the large amount of common interest shared by all the group.   (Mary Rawnsley, Clerk Typist, International Office)

At Park Lane College we have endeavoured to ensure that this learning curve is recognised formally. Too many colleagues have wished us a 'happy holiday' before leaving for an overseas visit. To resolve this issue, colleagues at Park Lane College worked together to develop a trainers' transnational work experience module and qualification, accredited through West Yorkshire OCN, which identified the new competencies skills and experience achieved on a transnational visit. This ensured that the staff development resulting from an overseas visit could be officially recognised within the Investors in People (IIP) accreditation, therefore accepting the work undertaken by staff in participating in such activities. Why should enthusiastic and committed staff suffer at the hands of others who lack the understanding of the added value of these visits?

Lessons learned

If a college is serious about integrating the European dimension into lifelong learning the college must have a written European/international strategy supported by an action plan that is constantly reviewed. The college must know what it wants from the European dimension, and commit this to paper and the website to inform everyone else too! The strategy must be approved by the principal and senior management team, and also – and more importantly – the college's governing body. Operational staff, whether a dedicated resource within a central European/international office, or located in operational departments, need to have a framework against which they can map their proposed activities. European/international activity must be owned by the whole college, not by individuals. This strategy and action plan should be reviewed on an annual basis, and again matched against the college's overall mission and corporate development plan. How does the European/international strategy support and add value to the college's core business? Action plans need to be reviewed against agreed performance indicators – otherwise how do you measure success, identify failure or calculate impact? Not all European/international activity is going to be successful, and therefore should not be continued. Failure, as well as success, should be identified.

In the very early stages of development it is useful to carry out an audit of European/international activity to inform the decision-makers as to current status. This activity will help identify the other 'enthusiasts', with whom it is possible to develop future activity. Start small to develop experience, and expand as confidence and commitment in college grows. Do not chase money.

A college does need to invest in a resource to support the development of the European/international dimension. However, it should not fall into the trap of thinking that being 'European' leads to 'lots of dosh'. Funding from European grants is available to support on a co-financing basis specific, targeted projects – EU grants do not provide 'profit' and will not always cover staffing and overheads. Too many colleges place an 'income generation' burden on their European co-ordinators, and in too short a timescale – 12 months is not feasible or appropriate. Development can take 18–24 months when starting from a clean sheet of paper. Integrating the European dimension does not always need extra cash – much can be achieved within the curriculum if curriculum managers are keen to integrate the European dimension particularly into full-time courses.

The days of 'Europe' being a bolt-on are long gone. Life and business in the UK are subject to European legislation, the single market is the 'home' market and must be recognised as such. In many ways, whether we join the 'Euro' is irrelevant from a learning perspective, as all businesses trading outside of the UK need to understand how to work with the 'Euro'. Central and local government have been dealing with ECU and now Euro for the last 25 years!

So what is the role of your European/international co-ordinator? It totally depends on your strategy and action plan but can include a range of activities:

- Setting up a European resource centre to provide information in regard to:
  - information/documentation relevant to curriculum managers;
  - a college-based database of transnational partners, their organisations and function;
  - guidance on EU funding available;
  - directory of college European/international projects;
  - information to support businesses;
  - maintenance of the college website relevant to European/international activities and projects.
- Co-ordination of all European/international projects ie, 'the one-stop European/international shop'.
- Development and implementation of systems and processes with local and transnational partners, to safeguard those undertaking visits, exchanges and work placements in another country.
- Provision of support services to local businesses.
- First contact in college for all transnational partners.
- First contact in college for all external liaison with the European Parliament, European Commission, European technical assistance offices, national government departments and co-ordination units, regional government, Regional Development Agencies and local government in regard to 'European projects' ie, the one-stop shop.

- Supporting the operational departments in the writing and submission of European funding applications and delivery of successful projects (but not owning the project themselves).

- Leading the cross-college internal network to assess progress to date on activities, review the action plans, support the development of new projects that match the strategy, review the strategy and recommend amendments to meet the ever-changing external environment and measure performance against the performance indicators included within the action plans.

- Represent the college on local, regional, national and transnational committees, networks and working groups as appropriate, eg FE regional networks, FEDA Euronet.

The list does not end here. Some colleges' European/international strategies include international student recruitment, requiring an element of marketing expertise. The essential ingredient in determining the role of this individual and the support team is the college European/international strategy, and for a college taking this work seriously it is not a part-time or temporary job. Continuous staff turnover in this post seriously damages the college's health.

Finally, what skills do you need for this work? Yet again this does depend on the strategy, but generic skills should include enthusiasm, energy, perseverance, tolerance, patience and a thick skin, and foreign languages can be useful too.

The key to successful embedding of the European dimension is 'partnership' and belonging to networks – not just transnational, but local or regional partnerships and networks. Being part of networks can be as simple as being on a national technical agencies database. Looking for partners? Contact the Central Bureau for International Training and Exchanges. Wanting to share experience or seek advice form other practitioners? Join the Learning and Skills Development Agency's 'Euronet', or regional FE Europe networks. Sharing experience, knowledge and ideas is the most empowering tool available for colleges. Recognising the complementary skills and services that local, regional and transnational partners bring can lead to larger, stronger partnership applications and projects, which ultimately have a greater impact on your target group. Remember – doing things differently does not mean doing them less well. Forget the days of 'information' means power – this is irrelevant with the European dimension. Sharing leads to new and improved projects and services, raising your organisation's profile, developing new ideas and contacts leading to new and improved projects and services!

16 'Perhaps' visions: rethinking European activities within a university school of continuing education

Keith Forrester

Introduction

Continuing education (CE) departments in British universities have not been the most enthusiastic players in European Union- (EU) funded projects in recent years. Quite a few departments, in fact, seemed to have shown no interest at all in such developments, which is strange. They would have been under the same pressure from senior management as other colleagues throughout the country to 'draw-down' European funds. In the lean, cash-strapped university environment of the mid-1990s, any means of relieving the financial constraints was to be grabbed with both hands! The sums of money available through the EU were so substantial that few universities could afford to ignore them.

Other, more 'sophisticated' pressures were at work in the early years of the 1990s that encouraged university staff to look seriously at European opportunities. The Economic and Social Research Council had opened an office in Brussels and was organising workshops on the Commission's framework programmes for research and technology development. Moreover, the 'international excellence' category in the Research Assessment Exercise signalled the importance to be attached to international work with colleagues from outside Britain. For those university adult and continuing educators really on top of things, there was always the 1991 European Commission's *Memorandum on Higher Education in the European Community*, which not only focussed on the particular role and contribution of higher education, but also raised a number of strategic issues relating to the nature and future direction of universities.

If there were a number of gentle and some not too gentle hints about getting involved in European activities in the early 1990s, there were also reasons why this could, at best, be postponed for a few years and at worse, be ignored altogether. Workload pressures were building up dramatically and the 'returns' from 'investing' in Europe were difficult to judge with any degree of accuracy. The sums of money involved for this or that particular project, while welcome, were in the main unlikely to detract from a 'business as usual' position. Moreover, even where there was the luxury of a European office within the university, its staff was unlikely to be familiar with the adult education aspects of EU-funded programmes (as in the case of the SOCRATES programme). Individuals, in other words, would have to plough through the seemingly huge reams of documentation on their own, in an attempt to make sense of what a particular programme was about.

Using the case study experience of the School of Continuing Education at the University of Leeds over the past 6–7 years, this article will argue that those university continuing educationalists who did risk the plunge into EU funded projects in the mid-1990s are well-placed today to benefit from those experiences.[1] Although these 'benefits' could, and probably do, include a range of immediate and valuable project management skills and experiences – such as budgetary control, developing and maintaining partnership relationships, evaluation studies and dissemination activities – this article will not focus on these areas. Instead, it focuses on the impact of these comparatively isolated European excursions on a range of more strategic issues about the nature and future direction of a university CE department over the next 5–10 years. The lessons of our European experiences, in other words, has contributed to a wide-ranging discussion amongst (many, but not all) colleagues about the type of continuing education or lifelong learning practice and institutional arrangements that we see unfolding in the future. The European experience, obviously, was not the only factor prompting these more strategic considerations, but it certainly was an important contributing measure.

This article illustrates and discusses how European issues have moved from the margins of the department's learning and research agendas in the early 1990s towards current discussions and planning that began to strategically situate the European agenda at the centre of important areas in the school's CE activities. The primary vehicle encouraging these discussions has been the various EU-funded projects (mainly SOCRATES) that involved school staff. The first section outlines those concerns and aspirations that shaped our 'European' thinking within the school in the early 1990s. The second part sketches our project experience before summarising, at the beginning of the new EU-funded programmes involving adult learning, the discussion in the school over the possible 'Europeanisation' of our activities. The final section raises a number of general issues that are likely to be common to most, if not all, educational agencies that have 'survived' European projects under the last round of programmes.

---

[1]The views expressed in this article reflect those of the author and do not express the 'official' view of the school.

The 'weak and fragile' situation in 1993

In the early 1990s our knowledge and experience at Leeds of EU-funded projects was extremely limited. We were aware of such projects and had, in the early 1990s been a partner in a TEMPUS project that, as a result of being forced to merge with another network and having our budget cut by 50 per cent, came as close as you can get to civil war within the polite circles of adult education! Our project lasted two meetings and was cancelled after the first year. A more successful early experience of European collaboration was a PHARE democracy project with partners in Slovenia and Ireland. This worked well and was useful in introducing us to the delights of the week-long audit visits from the Technical Assistance Office.

Such early involvement in EU-funded projects dove-tailed with our growing, although uneven, involvement with colleagues from other parts of Europe (and elsewhere). We had, for example, organised some four international conferences in the previous 6–7 years and were beginning to establish a confidence with particular individuals, their programme and research interests and their institutions, be they universities, trade unions, training agencies or non-governmental organisations (NGOs). Some of these organisations invited us to visit them, or to join their conference's organising group. We were, moreover, getting increasingly involved with some of the research networks within the European Society for Research in the Education of Adults (ESREA) and, domestically, were participants in the European network of the Universities Association for Continuing Education (UACE), which provided a useful forum for discussion and information gathering.

It was decided in 1992 to draw-up what we ambitiously called a 'European Plan' for the departments' work. A questionnaire to all staff was useful in identifying our existing links and relationships: the many gaps; the extent and nature of the linkages; the benefits and disadvantages staff felt would result from stronger European collaboration; the European languages available within the Department; and the constraints upon colleagues in strengthening our European involvement. The results were unsurprising and would have mirrored patterns elsewhere. In short, colleagues felt that their work would substantially benefit as a result of closer European collaboration, already had some relationships with individuals dotted around north and central western Europe, but saw 'time' and existing workloads as major constraints in getting further involved. Discussions of these conclusions at the departments' annual conference in 1993, resulted in the document being down-graded from a 'European Plan' to 'Consultative Notes'!

As the document noted, 'The overall level of Department involvement in European activities is too weak to risk jeopardising current relationships.' On a bolder note, however, the Consultative Notes did prioritise a number of geographical areas within the EU that either required consolidating and strengthening, or 'opening up a front' for the first time. Particular activities and organisations were identified for staff willing to slowly develop an awareness of European issues and possible relationships. Although not overtly ambitious, the Consultative Notes were a useful means of establishing some 'space' for European issues and in identifying this areas of work as an agenda issue for the school. A start had been made.

Project overload in Framework Five

By 1999 the Department was beginning to slowly recover from the frenetic project activity of the previous 4–5 years. Innocently testing the European waters had resulted in three SOCRATES projects, a LEONARDO project, an 'Innovative Programme' project (all of 2 years duration) and a European Social Fund research project. The department had been responsible for the co-ordinating or/and contractor responsibilities in all three SOCRATES projects and was co-ordinator in the LEONARDO programme. The learning curve was a steep one, especially given that one SOCRATES project had a university and a trade union/confederation from each of 12 countries.

We learnt a lot very quickly (and occasionally, painfully). For example, while the sums of money may look impressive, when shared out amongst the partners, everyone is in effect working for very little. There is the argument, and in some cases the evidence, that participation in an EU-funded adult education project actually costs the department or 'social partner' more than they receive. But we also learnt (thankfully) that you only involve yourself in a project where the tasks and activities are those which you were 'going to eventually get round to sometime in the future'. In other words, the projects provided some financial support and a disciplinary framework for doing things now, rather than having them on a never-never list. In our case, for example, it was the design and production of a number of 'flexible learning' modules and the resources to transfer these to an online format. In another, it was the design and development of a citizenship internet site or the extension to a European arena of a domestic research interest (into lifelong learning and universities) that was completed.

As well as these welcomed project 'deliverables', there were a number of other benefits. We were deepening our knowledge about, and extending our relationship with, other European colleagues, their institutions and their agendas. We shared the excitement of hearing, for example, how joint learning programmes involving trade union members from Denmark and Sweden were progressing and envisaged a strengthened 'Baltic Regions' learning project involving local trade unionists from different Baltic countries working together.

We enjoyed berating Rectors from august universities about their institutions' failure to address issues of access; social exclusion and lifelong learning, and all celebrated the signing of a historic first-ever 'Protocol' between a Portuguese university and the National Trade Union Confederation. The niggles about money, the incessant emails and the bureaucratic chores were soon forgotten! We were experiencing and working through what most of the EU-funded projects had been designed to do; namely, developing collaborative working relationships with other European partners, designed to establish a basis of trust, confidence and knowledge of each others situation, objectives and constraints.

Moving on: the new programmes

The lull before the staggered introduction of the new adult education programmes (LEONARDO and the new SOCRATES programme with its adult education strand GRUNDTVIG) provided an opportunity for all interested parties to reflect, rethink and, tentatively, plan ahead. Such a review however, at least in the British case, could take place within a much more encouraging context when compared to the early 1990s. European projects, for example, are now a familiar part of further and higher education's landscape (and revenue streams!). Many voluntary organisations are actively involved with various European partners and consultants await around every corner to steer those less confident through the often intimidating application pathways. Various workshops on European projects are now a familiar part of the conference circuit. And, of course, there has been the change of government which, in its own peculiar 'third way', has been a lot more encouraging and supportive of greater European involvement.

Towards the end of 1999 we produced a second discussion document entitled 'Developing our European work: Discussion Notes'. This document was a lot more confident. We were in the comparative luxury of suggesting that 'we might risk being a little bolder in our strategic thinking about the role and contribution of European projects to the future work and direction of the school' (p.2).

Our European experience had encouraged us to move from a pragmatic perspective in the early to mid 1990s to more strategic considerations at the end of the decade. It was not only our European project experience, however, that encouraged a more adventurous and strategic consideration of our 'relationship to Europe'. Individuals in the school had, for example, continued to play an active part in ESREA activities and were in a position to evaluate the concrete benefits of working closely over a number of years with colleagues from other European agencies. Moreover, an international research conference on 'work and learning' in September 1999 had involved a surprisingly strong European contingent of participants and reflected the school's involvement in a variety of formal and informal working networks developed in the previous years. The school had just completed a Masters course for Swedish civil servants, in partnership with two Swedish universities, which had been organised under the recently established Lifelong Learning Institute; a university-wide research institute based within the school. Finally, as the recent Discussion Notes document mentioned, the school is 'increasingly … centred around European issues such as lifelong learning, social exclusion, modernisation, partnerships and the restructuring of post-compulsory learning' (p.2).

A number of developments could be identified that pointed in the direction of the school needing 'to decide whether we continue as before or step up a gear'. 'If we choose the latter option', the Discussion Notes suggests, 'we need to reach some decisions about our future direction – about the type of school we want to be in 5–10 years' (p.4). The school has only recently begun these discussions. The questions underpinning the discussions are not the sort of questions that suggest straightforward answers, nor are they likely to be concluded within a neat and tidy period of time. They are the sort of questions that are periodically raised in the various and numerous 'business' meetings of any organisation. There is, however, a suggested urgency and framework to the discussions, set by the impending deadlines of the EU adult learning programmes. Identifying and applying for such programmes, which dove-tail into, or progress the school's strategic objectives, rather than simply meeting the interests of an individual or group within the school, would be greatly helped by some tentative consensus around these more strategic questions.

Just as the questions flowing from a consideration of 'what type of school we want to be in 5–10 years' are quite big ones; the conclusions are equally large in their consequences – and perhaps, quite radical. Is it, for example, a case of systematically integrating European concerns into our curriculum and learning materials, or is it a case of completely rethinking and, perhaps, reorganising the way we work within the school? Should we not be imaginatively considering loose working networks, involving various colleagues from various learning agencies in Europe as our pedagogic and research 'home(s)' (or subject specialist groupings)?

Within such a scenario, the school becomes more like a faculty that provides a coherence and strategic developmental perspective to the multiplicity of activities involving school staff (and possibly to network colleagues employed in other agencies/universities around Europe). Working with European colleagues around negotiated themes and agreed issues in learning and research initiatives *begins* the discussion of what we do and how we do it, rather than the other way around. Partnerships become the lifeblood of the work in the school, rather than an optional extra to be selected only if we have the time or inclination. Developing our own loosely associated European Schools of Continuing Education, based on a complex of interlocking networks, perhaps is the way forward. In one sense, it does not matter what the answers (if any) are to such questions. What is more important is the opportunity for envisaging possible scenarios around 'working in Europe'. We will, of course, still be chasing 'FTE's', worrying about our 'marketing strategy' and 'balancing the books', but 'perhaps' within a reformulated context that is more exciting, innovatory and European than before.

Similarly, it does not matter what answers to these 'European' questions we arrive at, if in the process we are forced to consider how our understandings and practices around 'Europe' relate to our wider international agenda. Where, for example, do our existing relationships and practices with colleagues in South East Asia, Africa or even North America, fit into our 'perhaps visions'? Are we not in danger, when considering Europe, of repeating the parochialism that we wish to move away from within our domestic situation? Perhaps.

Conclusion

The current policy context that bears down on adult education – such as 'widening provision', 'lifelong learning' and 'social exclusion' – has encouraged a critical re-examination of what we do and why. This re-examination is a small part of a larger change scenario that raises questions about what is to be understood as learning, the relationships underpinning this and the contribution of institutions, such as universities, to existing and future possibilities. Attempting to make sense of the changes, together with their numerous 'hidden' agendas, is an exciting but risky business. Those of us involved in 'post-compulsory learning' need to be part of these debates and pressures for reform. However, our own practices, assumptions and aspirations are far from satisfactory, irrespective of our institutional base. Outside of our own institutions, we remain, to a worrying degree, largely invisible. While we do have the potential 'to make a difference' across a number of different fronts and with a number of varied audiences, we are failing to meet this challenge.

The Leeds embryonic European experience in the 1990s has reinforced the urgency of reviewing what we are doing and where we want to be going. Discovering that there are other colleagues scattered throughout various countries who share your perspectives and ways of working, or have progressed considerably beyond this, is exciting. Imagining how these relationships can move beyond a limited, project-based duration raises far-reaching questions about the way we operate and why, in our departments and institutions. Perhaps we could have reached this point without participation in European projects. In making the projects work, however, there are the inevitable glimpses of a different future (or futures) are founded on relationships, decision-making processes and programmes that extend beyond the institutional limitations of our domestic base. Learners and learning, by necessity and design become 'European' and so reflect a more complicated, contested and messy reality. Perhaps.

The European Commission must be smiling gently to itself. Dangling a small number of incentives in front of the noses of adult learning providers has precipitated, or at least contributed towards, a wide-ranging discussion about 'how' and 'what' should be developed in the years ahead. And, at the centre of the discussions, is the issue of collaborative working relationships with other European colleagues. Few arguments, case-study experiences or 'dissemination' workshops could have proved so effective in situating 'Europe' at the centre of local discussions being undertaken in hundred of agencies across the region!

17   Reflecting on policy

Sue Waddington

In the early 1990s, leading policy-makers in the European Union (EU) recognised the significant challenges that were facing Europe. It was a time of high unemployment and low economic activity. The EU was in danger of failing to compete effectively with the other major world trading blocks, including the USA and Japan and the Far East, which did not embrace the welfare state model of the majority of EU members. Jacques Delors spelt out the situation and proposed some solutions in his 1994 white paper *Growth, Competitiveness and Employment*. The paper addressed a range of issues and significantly stated that Europe's best asset was its grey matter – its collective brainpower. This paper paved the way for a development of European policies and programmes for lifelong learning.

The EU and lifelong learning 1994–99

During the 1994–99 period the EU embarked upon a variety of initiatives that emphasised the importance of lifelong learning to employment, competitiveness, social inclusion, equal opportunities, citizenship, the ageing population and technical advances in the work place. In 1996, the European Year of Lifelong Learning provided an opportunity to examine the research that demonstrated the link between investment in education and training and economic development. It also enabled many bodies from all member states to high light learning as a means to success.

These developments were not linear or always coherent. The co-ordination, organisation, dissemination and complementarily of the programmes and policies has sometimes been weak. Nonetheless, there has been a general acceptance and political agreement on the fundamental principle of the importance of lifelong learning to Europe's future. This has been demonstrated, most clearly by the European Commission's employment guidelines, agreed by all member states in 1997, which give the highest priority to learning. Each member state has made a commitment to draw up an action plan each year to meet agreed targets for the education and training of young people, and those who are unemployed. The guidelines and the targets have become more ambitious each year, and now include reference to the importance of lifelong learning to older workers. European policies and programmes to develop and sustain lifelong learning as part of a Europe of Knowledge will need to continue to be built upon in the next decades.

The powers of the EU

There are, however, strict limits to the powers of the EU, which are set down in the various treaties. Education and training policies and systems are the responsibility of the member states themselves, and not the EU. Instead, the EU can provide funding programmes to encourage a European dimension to education and training. It has done this mainly through the SOCRATES, LEONARDO and Youth for Europe programmes. Preparations for the second generation of these programmes (2000–06), was influenced by the development of policies on a 'Europe of Knowledge' and the recognition of the importance of lifelong learning. It is through its funding programmes and more limited voluntary agreements entered into by member states, that the EU has sought to influence the development of lifelong learning.

In contrast, the EU is able to impact more directly upon member states' social and employment policies. The Social Chapter, which has been in incorporated into the Amsterdam Treaty, allows policies determined at EU level, such as the 1998 agreement on the right to parental leave, to be transposed into legislation at member state level, and provides a formal policy negotiation role for the Social Partners (Trades Unions and Employers). There is currently no definition of, or formal policy-making role for, the education partners in Europe.

Partly as a consequence of the lack of a formal policy-making role and the weakness of the Commission in the co-ordination of policies for lifelong learning, educators have tended to neglect the EU as a source of influence. Trades unions, employers and commercial organisations, and increasingly local and regional authorities and NGOs (non-governmental organisations) have actively lobbied and sought to inform themselves about and influence European policy and legislation, while educators and their institutions have seen the EU mainly as a potential source of funding for projects. However, the EU is a dynamic body, with expanding borders and developing powers and policies. The publication of the *Commission Memorandum on Lifelong Learning* in the autumn of 2000 and the subsequent debate suggests that it may now be time for educators to consider how and why to take a greater interest.

The benefits of EU-funded projects

European funding has been of considerable benefit to lifelong learning in all member states. Despite the administrative hurdles that need to be overcome, successful project bids have brought added value to those who take part and their institutions. The projects have enabled students and staff to work with new partners, widen their horizons, and provided opportunities to raise levels of cultural awareness, test out new approaches and learn and share ideas in a transnational context. In addition to the EUs flagship education and training programmes of SOCRATES, LEONARDO and Youth for Europe there are a range of existing and new programmes that provide opportunities for funding lifelong learning. These include the European Social Fund (ESF) and the new EQUAL programme, the 5th Framework for Research and Development, the European Year of Languages 2001, and the new Anti-Discrimination package. These opportunities have and will enable priority to be given to the education and training of target groups, including young people, women, the long-term unemployed, those vulnerable to exclusion, disadvantaged communities and asylum seekers, as well as the wider community.

The programmes are also aimed at developing new approaches to a range of educational challenges, including new information and communication technologies, sustainable employability, entrepreneurship, adaptability, equal opportunities, language learning, new areas of employment, active ageing and combating discrimination. They differ from national funding programmes because they aim to encourage transnationality, the testing of innovatory approaches that are relevant for dissemination at a European level and the development of European partnerships.

Education practitioners, whose main priority is to seek external funding for local projects, can overlook the benefits of European added value. However, the potential opportunity for spreading and embedding exciting approaches to address issues and problems that are common to European societies can be one of the most rewarding aspects of taking part in a European project. One such example is Adult Learners Week, which was pioneered by NIACE in the UK and subsequently attracted European funding, which led to its wider dissemination. The equivalent of Adult Learners Week now occurs in virtually all European countries, with the aim of encouraging, motivating and informing adults to continue or return to learning. New ideas have been developed and new partners have become involved, across the EU and beyond.

The partnerships formed in order to undertake a European project can also develop to provide the added value of sustainable links. Colleges and Universities in the UK are members of European networks, often set up with the main purpose of gaining funding, but which have developed in scope to include private enterprises and research institutes. They have provided opportunities to enrich the curriculum, support broadly-based exchange opportunities, exchange new ideas for research and development, and the sharing of good practice.

The wider picture

However, far greater benefits may be gained from Europe than those provided by taking part in the limited number of EU-funded projects. Firstly, we can learn a great deal from the education and training initiatives of other member states, which have been developed with little if any European funding. In

Denmark, for example a method known as the job rotation system is used to enable employees of private and public enterprises of all sizes to take paid secondment for education, training or family reasons, while their jobs are filled by unemployed people who receive initial and in-house training. In other Scandinavian countries, every employee is entitled to 2 weeks training leave each year. In France, there is an established network of universities of the Third Age and a growing network of 'second chance schools', for young people who have rejected or been excluded from the mainstream, but who are motivated by the most up-to-date technology and cultural opportunities. In Italy, increasing attention is being given to training for the 'third sector' labour market, with 'not for profit' organisations. In the UK, the introduction of Individual Learning Accounts and the University for Industry have attracted the Commission's attention and deserve greater dissemination.

Both EURYDICE (the European Education Information Network) and CEDEFOP (European Centre for the Development of Vocational Training) have some responsibility for the collection, analysis and dissemination of information about education and training policies, systems and initiatives. However, there is still a need for better, more accessible, and relevant methods of dissemination that involve and inform educational practitioners.

Secondly, to gain the maximum benefit from the EUs commitment to lifelong learning, there is a need for educators and their representatives to seek to be involved in the development and implementation of European policies and programmes. Traditionally, Trade Unions (TUs) and employers organisations have viewed the European institutions as a source of legislation and influence over member states, as well as a source of funding. However, educational bodies have been mainly concerned with the outcomes of the European decision-making processes that relate to eligibility for funding. This is also true of the non-statutory sector, where NGOs concerned with the social policy agenda are represented on a Social Policy Platform, which meets regularly with the Commission, follows policy proposals and lobbies MEPs. There is no equivalent Education Platform, although the Commission is considering whether to set one up.

It is the appropriate time for educators to consider how they can promote the European dimensions in lifelong learning. The new generation of European funding programmes for education, training and regional development (2000–06) give a higher priority to lifelong learning, which is seen as one of the key factors in meeting the global challenges that face European member states. The Commission's own *Memorandum on Lifelong Learning* (CEC 2000) set out a number of principles for debate in member states. There are many interested parties, which have and will seek to influence the further development and implementation of these policies, and provide analysis and wish lists for the future. Those involved in education should be prepared to enter the debate, and bring their experience of extending opportunities to the negotiations. Experience at local, regional or national level is of broader relevance, since many of the problems and opportunities that face teachers and learners are common to all European societies. Issues such as widening participation, accreditation, quality, achievement, access and curriculum concern all who are involved in education.

The decision-making processes

There are perceived and actual barriers to getting involved at a European level. European institutions suffer from the democratic deficit, and are seen, particularly in the UK, as overly bureaucratic and impenetrable. Problems caused by the lack of coherent policy, programme and implementation systems are frequently cited. Education practitioners taking part in European projects are aware of the administrative hurdles and sometimes contradictory rules, and generally learn to work round them, rather than considering how changes can be brought about.

The stated aim of the EU is transparency in decision-making, but it often fails to inform those who do not actively seek engagement, how it works. However, the basic processes are not very mysterious, and it is possible to exert influence at various stages and upon various players.

The Commission has responsibility of drawing up proposals for legislation, directives, programmes and policies that are within the remit of the EU as defined by the Treaties. These proposals take the form of official communications, which are then discussed by the relevant Committee of the European Parliament. The Committee appoints from within its number a rapporteur for each communication, whose task it is to consider and consult on the issue and, if appropriate, draw up amendments to the proposal. The Committee will discuss and further amend the proposal and vote upon it. The amended proposal is then taken to a plenary session of the full Parliament for one, two or three readings, and subsequently to the Council of Ministers for determination by qualified majority vote, or unanimity. The Commission and the Parliament can then further consider the outcome. This basic process has a variety of refinements, depending upon the subject and nature of the proposal concerned, which are defined by the treaties.

Many proposals are the subject of behind the scene negotiations involving member states, Commissioners, MEPs and others. Lobbyists and concerned organisations will also be seeking to influence the outcome, including representatives from TUs, employers and NGOs if they regard the proposals as significant to their interests.

During the period when the major funding programmes are being drawn up or revised, for example the Structural Funds in 1998–89, lobbying can be very intense, over the amount of resource, the division of that resource, and the plans for eligibility and implementation. Many of the funding programmes have recently been 'nationalised', which means that more decisions can be taken at the member-state level about how to allocate and manage the European resources they receive, within the limits determined by the EU. The moves towards regionalisation in the UK and elsewhere, has contributed towards a growth in the lobbying activities of local authorities and their regional offices in Brussels and the UK.

It is significant to note that no educational bodies sought to influence the shape or outcome of the negotiations surrounding the development of the legislation for the EUs education and vocational training programmes (SOCRATES II and LEONARDO II), for the period 2000–06, despite the problems of the previous programmes and the need for improvements.

Educators with knowledge, influence and a European dimension

The reasons why educators should seek influence are important. Europe provides opportunities to learn from our partners in other member states; it funds innovation, and it is developing policies that place learning at the centre of economic and social models. It is considering the role of the individual, the employer, the trade union, the community, the university, the education provider, and the member state in the learning process. There are many potential partners and there are many potential sources of influence. Those involved in education, as managers and practitioners should not ignore the influence or relevance of the European dimension, if they want to help to shape the future direction of policies.

In brief, it is necessary for educators to gain knowledge and access to networks that have the ability to influence events, and provide sources for the exchange of ideas. Knowledge about current developments, existing practice, new programmes and emerging ideas, can be gained from a variety of sources. Regional MEPs (whose names and addresses can be found by contacting the party political offices) should be able to provide information and be prepared to speak, or arrange regional meetings on Europe and educational topics. Staff in the Regional Offices in Brussels (funded by Local Authorities and LSCs/LECs or RDAs) can provide regular and up-to-date information. Both the EC and the Parliament have offices in London, which will provide literature on EU policies and programmes, and access to expert speakers. The EUs website is a rich source of information, which leads into the work of the different Directorate Generals of the Commission. Two DGs are of particular relevance: the DG for Employment, Industrial Relations and Social Affairs, and the DG for Education and Culture. In addition CEDEFOP and EURYDICE provide a wealth of data.

It is possible to seek knowledge about particular specialisms from amongst these sources, whether ones interest is in a curriculum area, such as information technology; a particular learning group, such as women; or in a particular region, such as one facing the challenge of economic change. Individuals, institutions and groups who acquire the information will gain useful knowledge about new programmes and funding opportunities, initiatives and potential partners, and matters under consideration.

It is also possible to visit the Parliament and Commission in Brussels, meet with the relevant Commission staff and MEPs and listen to the debates in Committee. Such visits can be arranged by MEPs and Regional Offices, or by intermediaries, such as TUs or professional organisations. Relatively few UK educators make visits of this kind, but they are useful to enable face-to-face contact with the relevant officials and politicians, and to experience the way that the processes and the players work.

Having gained knowledge about the current and emerging ideas on the European dimensions of lifelong learning, the decision-making process and the institutions involved, the opportunity to seek to influence events might be sought. One can seek to influence the outcome of Commission proposals and the longer-term strategy as an individual, or more powerfully as a member of a group, such as a TU, professional organisation, NGO, European network or association. This can be done by engaging with MEPs, Commission staff or the relevant UK government's representative. On Commission proposals under consideration, alternative ideas for amendments can be submitted, position papers prepared and circulated and the relevant representatives briefed.

The Commission is considering whether to provide more opportunities for European education associations to engage in organised debate, initially on issues related to the SOCRATES programme, and around its *Memorandum on Lifelong Learning*. If a European education platform were to be established for this purpose, its remit could develop to extend to longer-term strategy considerations. The associations involved would ideally, like the European TUs and employer's bodies that are recognised, be transnational in their membership. It is therefore important that UK-based education bodies take their European links seriously and engage in discussions with their European partners, since this may bring a seat at the negotiating table in Brussels.

Taking part in such a process is a medium- to long-term commitment requiring patience and time. The benefits, however, are potentially almost limitless. Every renegotiation of the European Treaty has resulted in a growth in power of the European institutions. The significance of lifelong learning for Europe's future has been recognised. In addition to the current membership of 15 countries, 13 new applicants are waiting in the wings and preparing for membership. Educators who are passionate about learning and its place in building tolerant, peaceful and successful societies and communities, should no longer ignore the European dimension, but be prepared to get involved.

References

CEC (2000) *Memorandum on Lifelong Learning*, Directorate General for Education, Youth and Culture, Commission of the European Communities

Section V
Where to find out more

18   Promoting lasting change through evaluation

Jane Field

Monitoring and evaluation are integral components of most European Commission programmes. Increasingly, those responsible for managing the programmes, and National Agencies in particular, are looking for evidence that projects take evaluation and monitoring seriously. But evaluation is not just a means of meeting an externally imposed requirement. It can also be a means of making your own work more effective.

To make the most effective use of evaluation in maximising the benefits of your project, the view taken in this chapter is that, whether the evaluation is done internally or externally, it should be a formative process. In other words, evaluation should contribute to the learning and development of a project. Realistically, a summative evaluation approach (at the most basic level, informing the project management team and partners as to those areas where the project may be judged to have 'succeeded' or 'failed') is ultimately historical. In practice, people will be moving on to the next challenge, and it is vital that they are able to learn lessons from their previous experiences.

This brief chapter is designed to introduce project partners to the process of developing an evaluation strategy that meets both the external (summative) requirements while providing internal (formative) lessons. Drawing on my own experiences in a number of European projects, including serving as an external evaluator, it provides a series of checklists that partners might use when agreeing their project evaluation strategy.

External evaluation

The benefit of using an external evaluator is that they can acquire inside knowledge about all aspects of the work of the project, without being 'bogged down' by its day-to-day operations. Thus it is possible to encourage key players and participants to reflect on what is happening; thereby identifying good practice, enabling strategies to develop, and identifying areas of constraint or conflict. The evaluation will contribute to the learning process not only to the benefit of the project and the partners, but also (ideally) for the benefit of the project funders. In short, the external evaluator might be seen as a 'critical friend'. Do not forget that an external evaluator can be budgeted for as a sub-contractor within your project proposal.

An external evaluation process should consider the impact of the project, both for the project partners and any beneficiaries. The external evaluator will observe the extent to which objectives and outcomes as initially agreed are actually met during the lifetime of the project; and look at the added value for all stakeholders that is gained from participation in the project.

Appointing an external evaluator will not necessarily save the project members' time. All partners must recognise that they will need to take time to reflect and complete the tasks set by the external evaluator, in order to gain maximum benefit. In compensation, many projects that have used an external evaluator find that the evaluation process adds value to the project, and supports the project management team in the delivery of reports and in taking a broader perspective of the project. External evaluation can also clarify misunderstandings, or identify areas to which the project management and partners need to pay further attention.

The outcomes from a formative external evaluation process should include:

- Interim evaluation reports, which will contribute to the project review process and will identify potential challenges and consider opportunities for future development;
- A final evaluation report, which will support the project final report for the funders, and, amongst other issues, show to what extent the project has met the original objectives and programme criteria; address lessons learnt; and identify those elements of the project that may be transferable to future projects;
- Insight into the wider impact of the project (admittedly, this is often hard to measure with any accuracy until some time after the project has formally come to an end);
- Identification of good practice and constraints;
- An active contribution to the learning process;
- An opportunity for informal and formal discussion and review.

Questions that the external evaluator could address include:

- How was the project successful/not so successful?
- Is it worth continuing or imitating elsewhere?
- What is the impact of the project?
- Transferability of experience to future projects?
- How cost-effective was the project?
- Where next?

Stages of the evaluation process should include:

- Documentation review;
- Accessing basic data (eg questionnaires, focus groups, exercises);

- Interviews (face-to-face or telephone);
- Observation (eg of partnership meetings);
- Analysis;
- Reports;
- Presentations and review.

Areas within a project that can be evaluated include:

- Project partnership;
- Project outcomes;
- Transnational issues;
- Products;
- Process;
- Records;
- Dissemination activities;
- Quantitative targets;
- Qualitative targets.

Internal evaluation and monitoring

Some projects prefer to carry out their own evaluation and monitoring procedures, or to carry out internal monitoring alongside an external evaluation. The advantages of a purely internal evaluation are that it saves money from the budget that can be allocated to project development and implementation. If one of the partners has expertise and experience in evaluation techniques it may indeed be appropriate to ask them to take on the role of internal project evaluation. If no partners currently have such expertise, it may be possible to build the costs of training in evaluation methods into the budget.

Internal evaluation and monitoring can take place at a number of levels, starting from the routine business meetings that oversee the project's development. One of the easiest, but most beneficial, evaluation tasks is to ask all partners to complete a simple evaluation pro-forma at the end of each meeting. Typical questions to include are:

- Expectations from the meeting (best completed at the start of the meeting)?
- Extent to which the expectations were met?
- What was learnt during the meeting?
- What was enjoyed/not enjoyed?
- What does each partner intend to do following the meeting?

Such a questionnaire not only encourages partners to reflect (albeit briefly) on the meeting; but also provides a pointer for the project management team, both for post-meeting follow-up activity, and in the planning of future partner meetings. Recorded notes of the responses can also provide useful evidence for reporting to external bodies.

Other areas to be taken into account when carrying out internal project evaluation and monitoring are:

Setting targets

a) Quantifiable targets, for example the number of:
   - Completed surveys;
   - Participants involved;
   - Dissemination activities;
   - Practical outcomes.

b) Time-based targets:
   - Were tasks completed on time?
   - Were deadlines met?
   - Did partners respect deadlines imposed in respect of consultation and contributions?

Project objectives

- How were objectives arrived at, and do all partners feel the same sense of 'ownership'?
- To what extent was each project objective achieved?
- What is the outcome of achieving the objectives?
- If problems occurred what mechanisms and strategies were employed to continue the momentum of the project?

Resources and value for money

- Was the original budget allocation appropriate to need, or was it reviewed and revised?
- Were any additional resources generated?
- In what ways was the project value for money?
- What tangible benefits were gained in relation to the total costs?

Problems experienced when monitoring projects internally

- Defining objectives;
- Agreeing roles;
- Setting targets;
- Planning the evaluation strategy;
- Collecting baseline data;
- Agreeing reporting procedures;
- The balance between formative and summative evaluation.

There may also be tensions within the partnership between those charged with evaluation and those who feel themselves the objects of evaluation, particularly if the latter are being criticised (or think they are).

Concluding comments

Evaluation is best treated as something that can balance two sometimes conflicting demands: it is a tool for meeting requirements for external account-ability, while providing a platform for organisational learning. No two projects are ever exactly alike, and no single set of checklists can do more than identify some of the key questions.

In the end, the core of evaluation is to be found in the word itself. It is a way of placing a value upon what is being achieved, and identifying the impact and added value as a result of the activities being undertaken. Hopefully, it can also be about valuing the project, both in terms of the processes involved and the results achieved during the lifetime of the project. The evaluation may provide evidence that there is need for further development work in this area – which could directly support a proposal for further project funding. Further-more, the evaluation process can also contribute to focusing the partner's ideas about what will continue to be implemented or further developed as a result of the project findings and activities once project funding has come to an end.

19 European resources on the web: an annotated list

John Field[1]

European institutions have developed a strong presence on the internet. As a result, the web offers ample resources to any adult educator wishing to explore the European dimension. This chapter lists some of the most important. For most purposes, I find that these are more helpful than any print materials, as they tend to be much more up-to-date, and usually offer contact addresses that allow me to get in touch directly with requests for further information etc.

Let me offer a couple of words of caution. You have to be prepared to do some surfing of your own. Like any website, these can change, and new ones can come online. Moreover, they are only a selection from the hundreds of online resources that are potentially available. Any decent search engine should help you overcome any challenges caused by these problems. You can also trace further materials, if you want them, by following up the 'links' that many websites contain.

Websites for the UK Government

Central Bureau for International Education and Training
The Central Bureau is funded by the UK Education Departments and the Department for International Development. It serves as the UK's national agency for most of the SOCRATES programme, including the GRUNDTVIG action on adult education.
www.britishcouncil.org/cbiet

DfES LEONARDO unit
Has a mailing list for information, pamphlets and useful publications, including advice on dissemination, putting together interim and final reports, etc. They hold conferences for promoters and would-be promoters, both in London and in regional centres, and participate in the LEONARDO Monitoring and Evaluation Seminar series.
www.leonardo.org.uk

[1]Although I take full responsibility for the selection of websites, and the accompanying details and commentary, the websites here were compiled on the basis of advice and information from all the contributors to this volume, and I wish to express my gratitude to those colleagues who guided my choices.

DWP EQUAL Unit

EQUAL is a Community Initiative designed to test out new ways of combatting discrimination and exclusion through transnational partnership activities. This official website is maintained by ECOTEC on behalf of the Department for Work and Pensions, and provides contact details and other information across the UK. It includes a brokerage service, where you can register your own organisation's details and interests and search for potential partners.
www.esfnews.org.uk/equal

European Commission Representation in the UK

The European Commission has offices, called Representations, in all the member states of the EU. The main UK office is in London with smaller ones in Belfast, Cardiff and Edinburgh. The staff are usually extremely approachable, and most helpful in providing advice and information on all aspects of the EU. The website gives details for all four UK offices.
www.cec.org.uk/about/index.htm

European Social Fund UK website

Provides official information from the Department for Work and Pensions and gives links to ESF contacts across the UK. Among other resources, you will be able to access the DWP's *ESF Newsletter.*
www.esfnews.org.uk

UK Office of the European Parliament

The European Parliament's office in the UK provides information to the public, the media, Government, regional agencies and the business community about the role and activities of the Parliament and the EU more generally.
www.europarl.org.uk/index.htm

UK SOCRATES – ERASMUS Council

The Council is the UK national agency for the ERASMUS higher education (HE) exchange action of the SOCRATES programme.
www.erasmus.ac.uk

UK Research Office

Established with an office in Brussels in 1991, UKRO is an information and advice service on EU funding for research and HE. It is jointly funded by the six UK Research Councils and the British Council and receives subscriptions from over 110 UK research organisations.
www.ukro.ac.uk

Websites – European Commission and its agencies

CEDEFOP (*Centre pour la développement de la formation professionelle*)

CEDEFOP is an agency of the European Commission charged with conducting research and analysing information on policy and practice in the field of vocational training, with the aim of helping inform policy-makers and practitioners.
www.cedefop.gr

CORDIS

Funded by the European Commission, this is the website providing comprehensive and generally up-to-date information on the Community Research and Technology Development programmes.
www.cordis.lu/en/home.html

EQUAL

EQUAL is a Community Initiative, funded by a top slice on the ESF, to test new ways of tackling discrimination and inequality experienced by those in work and looking for jobs It works through 'development partnerships' with the public, voluntary and business sector (in particular SMEs), who form links with at least one partnership from another country and engage with a network of others dealing with the same theme across Europe.
www.europa.eu.int/comm/employment_social/equal/equal.cfm

European Bureau for Lesser Used Languages

Created in 1981, and largely funded by the EU, the Bureau speaks on behalf of the more than 40 million EU citizens who speak a language other than the main official language of the State in which they live. This covers what the Bureau calls 'autochthonous' languages (including Welsh, Irish and Ulster-Scots, in the case of the UK), and not languages used by what it defines as more recent 'migrant' groups (such as Gujerati, Hindi, or Urdu). Its activities include study visits and support for publications.
www.eblul.org/infoeblul1.htm

European Commission

EUROPA, the official website of the EU and its institutions. Gives access to home pages for the European Parliament, and the Directorates General of the European Commission. You can also access relevant speeches, press releases and discussion documents on the site.
www.europa.eu.int/ comm/index_en.htm

The European Foundation for the Improvement of Living and Working Conditions

One of the European Commission's agencies, based in Dublin and concerned with sponsoring research and information concerning living and working conditions, which can include aspects of education and training. Also has a mailing list for their free updates.
www.eurofound.ie

European Social Fund

Official website for ESF can be found on the home pages of the Directorate General for Employment and Social Affairs.
www.europa.eu.int/comm/dg05/index_en.htm

European Training Foundation

The ETF is an agency of the European Commission charged with contributing to the process of vocational education and training reform that is currently taking place within its partner countries and territories. It also provides technical assistance to the TEMPUS programme.
www.etf.eu.int

EURYDICE

EURYDICE, funded as part of SOCRATES, is the European Commission's education information network in Europe. It produces readily comparable information on national education systems and policies.
www.eurydice.org

GRUNDTVIG

The GRUNDTVIG Action is part of the European Commission's SOCRATES programme, and is aimed at enhancing the European dimension of lifelong learning. It supports a range of activities designed to promote innovation and the improved availability, accessibility and quality of educational provision for adults, by means of European co-operation.
www.europa.eu.int/comm/education/socrates/adult/home.html

LEONARDO DA VINCI

LEONARDO is the European Commission's programme for vocational training. It supports innovative transnational initiatives for promoting the knowledge, aptitudes and skills necessary for successful integration into working life and the full exercise of citizenship, and affords scope for links with other Community initiatives – particularly the SOCRATES and Youth programmes – by supporting joint actions.
www.europa.eu.int/comm/education/leonardo_en.html

LEONARDO – National Agencies

A list of national agencies for LEONARDO, both within the UK and elsewhere, can be found on the European Commission's website.
www.europa.eu.int/comm/education/leonardo/leonardo2/nalist2.html

LINGUA

LINGUA is part of the European Commission's SOCRATES programme concerned with the promotion of language teaching and learning. It encourages and supports linguistic diversity throughout the EU; contributes to an improvement in the quality of language teaching and learning; and promotes access to lifelong language learning opportunities appropriate to individuals' needs.
www.europa.eu.int/comm/education/languages/actions/lingua2.html

MINERVA

The MINERVA Action forms part of the European Commission's SOCRATES programme, and seeks to promote European co-operation in the field of open and distance learning (ODL) and information and communication technologies (ICT) in education.
www.europa.eu.int/comm/education/socrates/minerva/ind1a.html

Official Journal of the European Communities

Published daily in 11 languages, the journal contains all calls for proposals, as well as copies of all EU legislation. Not a light read, but it is where the voice of power is recorded!
www.europa.eu.int/eur-lex/en/oj

Partnership between the Council of Europe and the European Commission for Training and Youth

In November 1998 the Commission and the Council of Europe signed an agreement to co-operate in the field of youth worker training. Since then, it has produced a number of attractive training publications (T-Kits) and the magazine *Coyote* was launched. Currently the T-Kits cover themes such as Organisational Management; Methodology in Language Learning; Project Management; and Intercultural Learning. It has also developed courses on European Citizenship and Training for Trainers. Each of these might easily be adapted for use with groups such as adult learners interested in community development and active citizenship.
www.coe.fr/youth/english/partnership/new/what.htm

SOCRATES

SOCRATES is the European Commission's education programme. Involving around 30 countries, not all of them members of the EU, it is mainly concerned with promoting European cooperation through mobility and exchanges, joint

projects, European networks, and comparative analyses. Its specific actions include GRUNDTVIG (adult education) and MINERVA (open and distance learning).
www.europa.eu.int/comm/education/socrates.html

SOCRATES – National Agencies

National agencies for SOCRATES are available on the European Commission's website.
www.europa.eu.int/comm/education/socrates/nat-est.html

TEMPUS

TEMPUS (the Trans European cooperation scheme for HE) is an EU programme. It was adopted by the Council of Ministers of the EU on 7 May 1990 and was extended for the third time on 29 April 1999, until 2006 (TEMPUS III).
www.europa.eu.int/comm/education/tempus/home.html

The Week in Europe

Weekly summary of news in the EU, as compiled by the Commission's representation in the UK. You can request delivery by email.
www.cec.org.uk/press/we

Websites – other international bodies

European Association for the Education of Adults

EAEA exists to link and represent European organisations directly involved in adult learning. Originally the European Bureau of Adult Education, it was founded in 1953 by representatives from European countries. Its primary membership consists of NGOs (including NIACE) whose principal aim is the education of adults, and it works through national co-ordinating bodies for adult learning.
www.eaea.org

Adult Learning Information Centre Europe

The ALICE database was funded under the European Commission's SOCRATES programme. It provides information on the work of non-formal education providers in the EU.
www.alice.eaea.org/index.html

Electronic Training Village

The Electronic Training Village (ETV) has been online since July 1998. Associated with CEDEFOP (see above), ETV creates a community of policy-

makers, researchers and practitioners in the field of vocational education and training (VET) in Europe and encourages dialogue and the exchange of knowledge and experience. Very user-friendly!
www.trainingvillage.gr

European Association for Institutional Research

EAIR brings together professionals in HE management, and academics researching HE.
www.org.uva.nl/eair/index.asp

European Basic Skills Network

EBSN is a partnership of national agencies with a responsibility for basic skills in six member countries. It has been set up to build a European basic skills network, share information, tackle social exclusion, establish a network of national organisations, promote basic skills strategies and influence national and EU policy.
www.eurobasicskills.org

European Bureau of Library, Information and Documentation Associations

EBLIDA is an independent non-governmental and non-commercial umbrella association of national library, information, documentation and archive associations and institutions in Europe. It focuses on issues such as copyright, culture, telematics, central and eastern Europe, information society related matters and information technology.
www.eblida.org

European Disability Forum

EDF – or FEPH (Forum européen des personnes handicappés) – was created in 1996. It represents disabled people in dialogue with the EU and other European authorities. Its mission is to promote equal opportunities for disabled people and ensure disabled citizens' full access to fundamental and human rights. Membership includes the national councils of disabled people from the 15 EU countries, plus Norway and Iceland, representing the national disability movements. There are also organisations representing different disability groups and campaign interests in Europe. A valuable source of direct information, interpretation and advice.
www.edf-feph.org

European Distance Education Network

An association open to networks, institutions and individuals, EDEN was established in 1991. It fosters developments in distance education through the provision of a platform for co-operation and collaboration between a wide range of institutions, networks and individuals concerned with distance education in Europe.

www.eden.bme.hu

European Educational Research Association.

EERA fosters the exchange of ideas and collaboration amongst European researchers, promotes research collaboration, and offers advice on educational research to European policy-makers, administrators and practitioners. Its specialist networks include groupings of researchers into vocational education and training (VETNET), inclusive education, open and distance learning, and HE.

www.eera.ac.uk

European Parliament – Committee on Culture, Youth, Education, the Media and Sport

As well as all aspects of education policy, the Committee is responsible for youth exchanges, the European Voluntary Service, the audiovisual industry and the cultural and educational aspects of the information society, and the dissemination and safeguarding of Europe's cultural heritage.

www.europarl.eu.int/committees/cult_home.htm

European Parliament – Committee on Employment and Social Affairs

The Committee is responsible for advising the Parliament, and drafting proposals, in the field of employment and social affairs. As well as vocational training policy, this includes equal opportunities, the social dialogue and the ESF.

www.europarl.eu.int/committees/empl_home.htm

European Prison Education Association

EPEA is an independent association representing teachers, trainers, librarians , administrators, managers and other professionals who work in prisons or whose work is concerned with promoting and developing education and related activities in prisons throughout Europe in accordance with the recommendations of the Council of Europe.

www.users.tibus.com/epea

European Research and Development Institutes of Adult Education

ERDI is a Consortium of European research and development institutes of adult education, serviced by the German national adult education association. It functions as a European network of national institutes active in research and development in adult education.

www.die-frankfurt.de/erdi

European Society for Research into Adult Education

ESREA is a membership organisation, comprised of both individual and organisational members. The website includes details of the specialist networks through which much ESREA activity is undertaken.
www.helsinki.fi/jarj/esrea

European Trade Union College/AFETT

The European Trade Union College (ETUCO) and the Association for European Training of Workers on the Impact of New Technology (AFETT) together form the training services department of the European Trade Union Confederation (ETUC – see below).
www.etuc.org/etuco/default.cfm

European Trade Union Confederation

The ETUC seeks to influence the EU by making direct representations to the various institutions (Commission, Parliament, Council), and by ensuring trade union participation in advisory bodies (including the Economic and Social committee, where most members of the Workers' Group comes from trade unions affiliated to the ETUC). The ETUC also engages with employers at European level through the 'social dialogue'.
www.etuc.org/default.cfm

European Universities Continuing Education Network

EUCEN was founded in 1991. It is represented on a number of committees and advisory panels at European level and provides experts and expert teams for international projects and consultancy to universities wishing to develop continuing education. Through conferences, projects and networking activities it provides opportunities for staff and curriculum development, sharing of best practice and development of international contacts among those involved in university continuing education.
www.eucen.org

European University Association

Formed in 2001 from a merger of two existing umbrella associations, EUA is now the main representative body for university level institutions in Europe.
www.unige.ch/eua

European Women's Lobby

The EWL is the largest co-ordinating body of national and European non-governmental women's organisations in the EU, with over 2,700 member associations in the 15 member states. Its goal is to eliminate all forms of discrimination against women and to serve as a link between political decision-makers and women's organisations at EU level.
www.womenlobby.org

Platform of European Social Non-Governmental Organisations

Established in 1995 with the aims of building an inclusive society and promoting the social dimension of the EU. It brings together over 1700 direct member organisations, associations and other voluntary bodies at local, regional, national and European level, representing the interests of a wide range of civil society. Ensures a wide circulation of information on EU activities and policies to its members at national level.
www.socialplatform.org

Towards a European Learning Society

The TELS project started in 1999 as a network of six cities, and now includes more than 80 communities across Europe (including Birmingham, Edinburgh, Sheffield and Southampton). Funded under the GRUNDTVIG action, TELS focuses strongly on adult learning as a core dimension of the learning region.
www.noesis.se/tels/index.cfm

Thematic Network Project in University Continuing Education

THENUCE is a trans-European mapping exercise sponsored by EUCEN (see above).
www.fe.up.pt/nuce

Union of Industrial and Employers' Confederations of Europe

UNICE is an 'umbrella' organisation representing national business associations across Europe. It is a formal party to the social dialogue, and carries out lobbying and other activities intended to influence EU policy on matters of interest to its members.
www.unice.org

4. Also worth checking out...

AONTAS

AONTAS is Ireland's national association of adult education. The website also includes links to other bodies in Ireland that are active in the field of adult learning.
www.aontas.com

Council of Europe

The Council of Europe is not to be confused with the institutions of the EU. Although all the EU's members belong to the Council of Europe, and its role encompasses some similar if looser aims of information sharing and cooperation, its membership is much broader, and it has no legislative powers. Historically, it has often taken a high level of interest in educational issues, including adult education and education for citizenship.
www.coe.int

Deutches Institut für Erwachsenenbilding

The Deutsches Institut für Erwachensenenbildung is the national German adult education association. Its highly informative website is in both English and German versions.
www.die-frankfurt-de

Lifelong Learning in Europe

Lline is a quarterly journal for those interested in adult learning across Europe. It originated as a SOCRATES project during the European Year of Lifelong Learning, and is published in Finland by the KVS Foundation and the Finnish Adult Education Research Society, with the Finnish Ministry of Education.
www.orivedenopisto.fi/kvs/kansanvalistusseura/lline.htm

Peuple et Culture

Major nationwide French adult education provider and lobbying body.
www.union@peuple-et-culture.org

Organisation for Economic Co-operation and Development

The 'rich nations club' was founded originally as a forum for economic co-operation among the European governments. Its membership has widened over the years and now includes Japan, the USA, Australia, Canada, Mexico and South Korea. OECD's Centre for Educational Research and Innovation has long been a stimulating source of policy thinking on lifelong learning.
www.oecd.org

UNESCO: Institute for Education

UIE (based in Hamburg) is one of a number of specialist UNESCO centres; it has a long track record of engaging with adult education and training.
www.unesco.org/education/uie

Index

Page numbers in **bold** typeface refer to tables